The Typological Imaginary

Circumcision, Technology, History

Kathleen Biddick

PENN

University of Pennsylvania Press

Philadelphia

Published by
University of Pennsylvania Press
Philadelphia, Pennsylvania 19104-4011

Library of Congress Cataloging-in-Publication Data

Biddick, Kathleen.
    The typological imaginary : circumcision, technology, history / Kathleen Biddick.
        p.   cm.
    ISBN 0-8122-3740-4 (cloth : alk. paper)
    Includes bibliographical references and index.
    1. Christianity and other religions—Judaism. 2. Judaism—Relations—Christianity.
3. Judaism (Christian theology)—History of doctrines—Middle Ages, 600–1500.
4. Typology (Theology)—History of doctrines—Middle Ages, 600–1500. 5. Graphic
arts—History—To 1500. 6. Antisemitism—Psychological aspects—History—To 1500.
7. Circumcision—Religious aspects. 8. Judaism in art. 9. Jews—Historiography.
I. Title
BM535 .B487   2003
261.2′6′09—dc21   2003050714

In memory of Bob Franklin,
dear companion

Contents

Illustrations

Introduction:
Typology Never Lets Go

This study grapples with an unsettling historiographical problem: how to study the history of Jewish-Christian relations without reiterating the temporal practices through which early Christians, a heterogeneous group, fabricated an identity ("Christian-ness") both distinct from and superseding that of neighboring Jewish communities. These Christian temporal practices insisted on identitary time, by which I mean the assumption that time can be culturally identical with itself. Early Christians straightened out the unfolding of temporality (with its gaps and vicissitudes) into a theological timeline fantastically based on two distinct but related notions. First, they posited a present ("this is now") exclusively as a Christian present. They cut off a Jewish "that was then" from a Christian "this is now." They also imagined a specific direction to Christian time. They believed that the Christian new time— a "this is now"—*superseded* a "that was then" of Israel. Such a temporal logic also enabled early Christians to divide up a shared scriptural tradition. Christians subsumed the Hebrew Bible into an "Old Testament" and conceived of this Old Testament as a text anterior to their New Testament. "Christian-ness" was thus affirmed by the repetitive cutting off of the old Jewish time from the new Christian time. Even though Christians shared literary genres and rhetorical conventions with pagan and Jewish contemporaries, their notion of supersession came to distinguish their reading and writing.[1] This book explores the stakes of this temporal model of Christian supersession.

The purported "secularization" of modernity, I contend here, has never overtaken this core Christian conception of supersession. Supersessionary thinking and notions of modernity are closely bound, and, I would argue, shape even the very terms of current debate among medievalists over the existence or nonexistence of antisemitism in the Middle Ages. At stake for me in this book is the belief that we cannot change the grounds of our historical narratives or ethically transform encounters with our neighbors unless we acknowledge and engage with the temporal fantasies and their supportive practices at the core of such "Christian-ness." Supersessionary notions, I posit, have rigidly bound the contexts in which Christians have encountered Jews, then and now. I term this captivating bundle of supersessionary fantasies about temporality the *Christian typological imaginary*. What follows analyzes the material vicissitudes of this Christian reduction of temporality into a binary of past and present. Put another way, by what technological means did "Christian-ness" fabricate itself and at what cost? And how does repetition of the Christian temporal imaginary fantastically shape historical contexts of encounter?

I explore supersessionary thinking from the relatively unfamiliar vantage point of the graphic technologies used in medieval texts and print sources from theological polemics to maps, trial transcripts, and universal histories. I seek to question how graphic technologies both embody and materialize supersessionary fantasies of cutting off the old Israel from the new Christian church. My study is thus also an intervention in cultural histories of technology, since it poses the relations of embodiment to disembodiment at the technological heart of imaginary fantasies. Repetition of such supersessionary practices (albeit unrecognized) extends even to contemporary psychoanalytic and postcolonial texts. I argue that even these self-critical approaches reflect the persistence of supersessionary thinking, even as they propose alternative ways of thinking about memory and temporality. Crucial to my study is the ethical and historical challenge of unbinding the typological imaginary, not to disavow theological difference between Christians and Jews, but rather to open up encounter to less constrained, less deadening historiographical habits of mind.

I do not need to emphasize that this book is less about documenting a record of Jewish-Christian relations than about imagining ways of thinking of new and rich temporalities that are not bound to the rigidity of supersession. Indeed, the book is about the risk of thinking about "unhistorical" temporalities—ones not about divisions between then and now, but about passages, thresholds, gaps, intervals, in-betweenness.[2] These unhistorical temporalities that do not use time as a utilitarian resource to ground identity are temporalities that can never be one.

Typology Never Lets Go

Let me exemplify the key terms of my argument through scrutiny of a graphic artifact. Figure 1 reproduces a page from the earliest printed

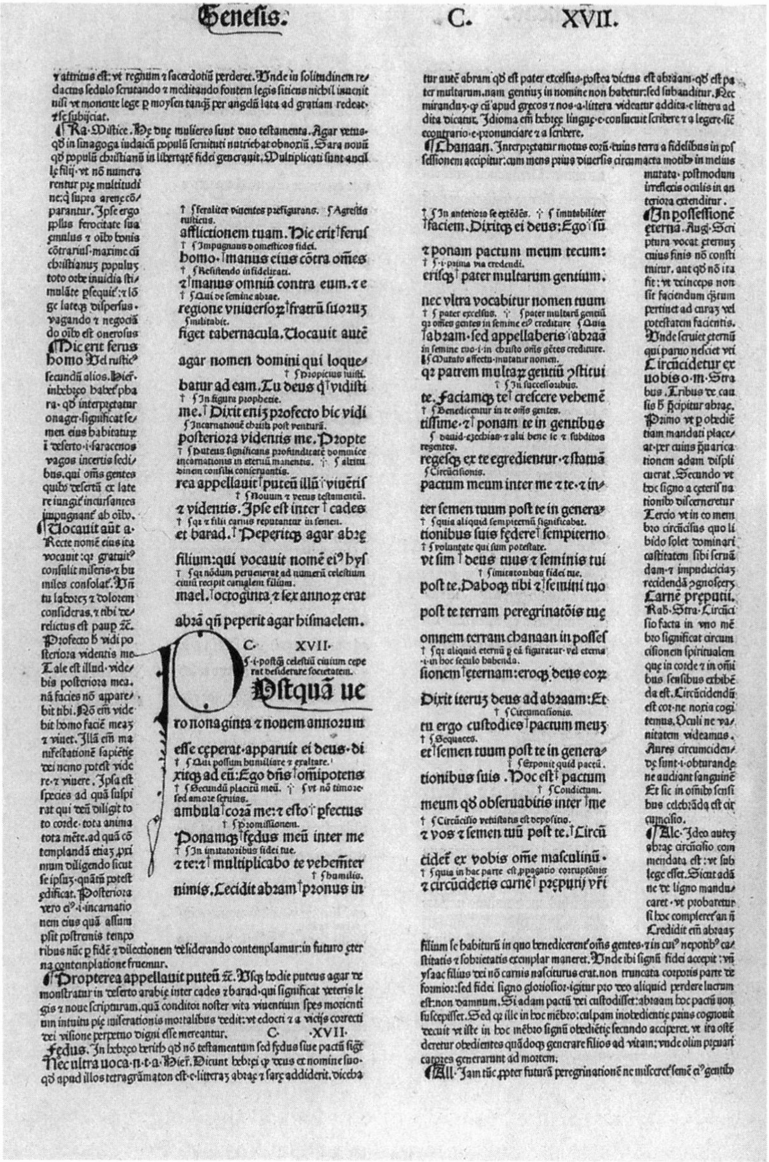

Figure 1. Genesis 17, *Biblio cum glossa ordinaria Walafrida Strabonis* (Strassburg, 1480), p. C. Courtesy of the Rare Books Division, New York Public Library, Astor, Lennox, and Tilden Foundations.

version (1480/81) of the medieval textbook version of the Bible
known as the *Glossa ordinaria*. By the time printers set the type, manuscript versions of the *Glossa ordinaria* had already been circulating in
this standardized layout for over three hundred years. Beryl Smalley,
the pioneer explorer of the Bible as a medieval schoolbook, reminds
us that the *Glossa* had an afterlife well into the Counter-Reformation.[3]
Later in this introduction, I shall have more to say about the formal
innovations worked out in the mid-twelfth century for graphic presentation of the Bible textbook. For now, I simply wish to draw attention to the center block of the page figured here.

Twelfth-century scribes and later printers reserved this space for
the biblical text, in this example, verses from Genesis 17, in which
God makes a covenant with Abraham. Another text, called the interlinear gloss, hovers above the Bible verses. For medieval students, this
gloss worked like an exegetical grid. It coordinated key terms and
figures selected from the text of the Old Testament with what Christian exegetes considered to be their figural fulfillment in key terms
and figures of the New Testament. We can see, for example, that over
the words of the Old Testament announcing the covenant of God with
Israel in the lower right-hand corner of the text block—*hoc est pactum
meum quod observabitis inter me et vos et semen tuum post te* (this is my pact
which you will observe between me and you and your seed after you),
the interlinear gloss inscribed the supersession of this covenant: *cir-
cuncisio vetustatis est depositio* (the old circumcision is deposed) and
coordinated the figure of Abraham with Christ as his figural fulfillment. These interlinear glosses, given their privileged placement
directly over the Old Testament text, functioned as pedagogical maps
to what is known as medieval typology or figural thinking.

Christian typology posits the theological supersession of the Christian Church over Israel. Christians believed that the New Testament
superseded the Hebrew Bible and redefined it as the Old Testament.
Exegetically it maps the figures of the Old Testament onto their fulfillment in the New Testament. Since the *Glossa ordinaria* was developed as a schoolbook—indeed, in 1179, Pope Alexander III ruled
that the Bible should not be taught without the Gloss—it had the
effect of standardizing the kind of typological thinking expressed in
the interlinear gloss. This is not to deny changing interpretative traditions, or other textbooks subsequent to the *Glossa ordinaria*, or even
radical disagreement about the value of glossing in the twelfth century. Smalley has rehearsed these debates in her indispensable work
The Study of the Bible in the Middle Ages, and more recently Philippe
Buc has elaborated on them in his *L'Ambiguïté du livre*. For my purposes it is precisely the mundane power of textbook typology in

such mechanical graphic layouts that is interesting. All the more so, since, as we shall now see, typological thinking continues to lure contemporary critical theorists, especially in their efforts to rethink historicism.

Scholars have regarded typological (also known as figural) thinking as one of the great achievements of late antique and medieval scriptural exegesis.[4] In his essay "Figura," written in Istanbul in 1944, Erich Auerbach traced the development of a specifically Christian form of figural thinking out of the recognition that "The Old Testament, both as a whole and in its more important details, is a concrete historical prefiguration of the Gospel" (44). He valued figural thinking because it supposed two events, Old and New, as historical—the historical Moses is a promise of the historical Christ who fulfills the figure of Moses. He contrasted the richness of such figural thinking with what he saw as the modern view of historical development: "whereas in the modern view the event is always self-sufficient and secure, in the figural interpretation the fact is subordinated to an interpretation which is fully secured to begin with: the event is enacted according to the ideal model which is a prototype situated in the future and thus far only promised" (59). As Auerbach formulated his study of figural thinking, a circle of French scholars around the Jesuit Henri de Lubac were also reviving medieval figural thinking as a resource for interpreting the Bible. De Lubac considered the relationship between the two Testaments as primary to exegesis and bemoaned historians who spent "vast storehouses of learning in vain" (224) because they failed to attend to the discontinuities between the Old and New Testaments: "the history of revelation also offers the spectacle of discontinuity that has no equal" (234). Both Auerbach and de Lubac insist on the supersession of the New Testament over the Hebrew Bible as central and distinctive to early Christian exegesis (in contrast to contemporary pagan and Jewish strands of figural thinking) and agree that Christian typology provided a productive and open-ended framework for interpretation.

This scholarly rejuvenation of medieval exegetical studies in the 1940s and 1950s profoundly influenced postmodern theoretical debates forty years later. Hayden White and Fredric Jameson, in particular, used Auerbach's vision of medieval figural thinking to champion new forms of historicism. Like Auerbach and de Lubac, White and Jameson envision figural thinking as a way of escaping from modernist notions of history based on rigid chronologies, notions of progress, and other forms of ahistorical thinking. Jameson's famous dictum—"always historicize"—is based on and draws its power from a figural move. Medieval figural thinking becomes with Jameson the figure of promise that his historicism fulfills. Yet, the richness of figural thinking so advocated by Auerbach, de Lubac, White, and Jameson constitutes for other scholars its unsettling historical problem. Michael Signer, for example, has concentrated on the interlinear glosses of the Pentateuch, as standardized in the *Glossa ordinaria*, because of their wide dissemination in the schoolbook. He argues that these glosses need to be apprehended as an institutionalized medium promoting anti-Judaism in the twelfth century. The close and repetitive graphic coordination of the names of Old Testament prophets with those who supersede them in the New Testament, *coupled* with their negative rhetoric of supersession, rendered the interlinear gloss as a form of graphic and rhetorical *substitution* for the Old Testament verses over which it was inscribed.

Jeffrey Librett, whose work considers the effects of Christian typological practices on Jewish-Christian dialogue, focuses on the figural process of doubling so cherished by Auerbach. Librett agrees with Auerbach that the distinctive aspect of Christian figural thinking is the supersessionary fabrication of texts of the Hebrew Bible into the Old Testament so that it (the Old Testament) might stand as prefiguration to the fulfillment of the New Testament. This supersessionary move produces Jews as the figures for the literal truth of Christians. However, it is never that simple, as Librett carefully shows. The fulfillment of a figure, say the Incarnation as the fulfillment of the Mosaic Law, can always also itself become prefiguration, in this case the Incarnation as prefiguration of the Last Judgment. Thus at the core of figural thinking is the fact that it is impossible to move from the event to its fulfillment without passing through doubleness. By this Librett means that figure and letter are both real and possible and that they therefore are always doubled and consequently can also be *self-reversing*. In other words, there is nothing to guarantee the irreversibility of figural thinking *except the theological notion of supersession*. Without the fantasy of supersession the figure of the Christian is always possibly the truth of the Jew. To forestall such a disturbing (to Christians) indistinction, normative Christian typological thinking binds itself to supersession. I am going to use the term the "Christian typological imaginary" to indicate those bundles of fantasies that bind "Christian-ness" to supersessionary notions. This imaginary must always work to ward off the shattering threat of typological reversibility. Indeed, the fantasy of supersession may be regarded as constitutive of the Christian unconscious, if we define the unconscious "as the locus of psychic activity whereby a human being becomes a 'subject' by metabolizing its existential dependency on institutions that are in turn sustained by acts of foundation, preservation, and augmentation."[5]

At this juncture it should be briefly noted that debates over Christian figural thinking are not confined to the academy. The Catholic Church continues to grapple with the question of how to think about a theology of the "Old Testament" that is not grounded in supersession.[6] Recent papal endeavors to open up Christian-Jewish relations show the difficulty of rethinking typology. In an address to the Jewish community of Mainz on November 17, 1980, Pope John Paul reemphasized that the "Old Covenant" had never been revoked by God. In 1985 a Vatican Commission for Religious Relations with the Jews had the following to say about typology:

From the unity of the divine plan derives the problem of the relations between the Old and New Testaments. The Church already from apostolic times (cf. 1 Cor. 10: 11; Heb. 10: 1) and then constantly in tradition resolved this problem by means of typology, which emphasizes the primordial value that the Old Testament must have in the Christian view. Typology however makes many people uneasy and is perhaps the sign of a problem unresolved. (224)

Nevertheless, in spite of good efforts, typology troubles Catholic catechisms, notably the recently authorized *Catechism of the Catholic Church* (United States Catholic Conference 1994). The catechism presents a typological understanding of the relations of the Jewish and Christian covenants. For instance, on the question of the constitution of the Bible, it asserts: "All Sacred Scripture is but one book, and that one book of Christ, because all divine Scripture speaks of Christ, and all divine Scripture is fulfilled in Christ" (141). Vatican studies have tried to exit typology by imagining both the Hebrew Scriptures and the New Testament as anti-types for the coming or return of the Messiah. This strand of eschatology is actually reminiscent of medieval expectations of a third age which envisioned a new hybrid chosen people (commingled of Christians and Jews) who would replace contemporary Christians as the chosen people. In a recent study of such millenarian thought, medieval historian Robert E. Lerner has characterized this vision developed by Joachim of Fiore (c. 1135–1202) as a more benign "path not taken" in the formation of Europe as a persecuting society. Yet such a path, Lerner observes, aggravates typology by adding the notion of progress to supersession: "As the first theorist of incremental progress in the West (and probably anywhere), Joachim spoke in terms of steady betterment extending into the future."[7] The Old Testament scholar Joseph Blenkinsopp takes the measure of the problem when he comments that "we [Christians] are as yet nowhere close to knowing how to write an Old Testament theology."[8]

Does the debate on typological thinking rehearsed so far seem to repeat, yet again, some version of the story of "timeless" enmity between Christians and Jews, even as scholars are working so hard to rethink these relations past and present? For example, late antique scholars now argue for the "twin birth" of rabbinical Judaism and Christianity and view the religions as siblings, thus sidestepping the question of theological imaginaries. Scholars of the medieval dias- pora reject monolithic understandings of religious and ethnic essence and eschew accusatory historical modes of describing medieval Jewish- Christian relations. They attempt to cultivate complex understand- ings of local differences as solutions to particular cultural problems that are never one-sided.

This book begins with the intuition that such hopeful new histori- cal models of Jewish-Christian coemergence and coexistence will not shift the ground of analysis unless they are accompanied by a thor- ough working through of the fantasy of supersession, or what I am calling the Christian typological imaginary. I will thus be making a cautionary argument in these pages about this promising new work.

The Typological Imaginary at Work

Let me open my argument with a reading of some current works of medieval scholarship that seek to rethink the historiography of Jewish- Christian relations. I wish to show how they stop short of being trans- formative, since they remain at what Eric Santner has called "the level of . . . mapping of more complex *symbolic* processes" (29) without ref- erence to the repetitive and machine-like aspects of the Christian typological imaginary. As psychoanalysis teaches us, unconscious mental activity is not organized around systems of meanings, beliefs, purposes, or epistemologies, but rather around a kernel that is not assimilable to biology or history (which is not to say that the kernel is a-natural or ahistorical). My reading suggests that the typological imaginary has persisted in these studies in spite of themselves. Only a questioning of the typological imaginary in tandem with such studies can be, I believe, transformative.

Medieval historians have mostly modeled the study of medieval Jewish-Christian relations at the symbolic level as a question of self and other and concomitant processes of inclusion and exclusion. Robert Moore's influential book, *The Formation of a Persecuting Society* (1987), remains paradigmatic.[9] He claims that newly emergent cleri- cal elites in late twelfth-century Europe, notably university scholars and administrators, secured their power by constructing and polic- ing new forms of outcastness. Jews became the Other for these medi- eval Christians. A strong reading of Moore (one that he himself has offered) argues that antisemitism is constitutive of the very formation of Europe. In so claiming, Moore conflates medieval bureaucratic networks with fantasy, failing to realize that they are not historically identical. Moore provides his readers with a bleak but paradoxically comforting historical narrative. He offers a temporal origin and a bureaucratic structure for antisemitism without raising any questions about the group pleasures being forged in the emerging networks of bureaucratic elites he traces. How does fantasy work to organize such bureaucracies in mechanical, repetitive ways? Since the bureaucratic networks are historically dynamic, so too, unhistorically, is the work of fantasy. Moore's thesis does not allow historians to think together these clerical, bureaucratic networks and the question of pleasure. Separating functionalism from fantasy, as Moore does, protects historians from thinking about the unhistorical, that which is troubling because it cannot be contained by the history of bureaucratic networks alone.

Moore's conflations have strongly shaped subsequent historiography. Through the 1990s medievalists responded both creatively and anxiously to Moore's paradigm of persecution.[10] Gavin Langmuir and Anna Sapir Abulafia have looked more carefully at clerical strategies for "christianizing" reason as clerics redrew the boundaries between the rational and the irrational over the twelfth century. They are interested in how intellectuals innovated the media of textbooks, polemics, preaching, and visual display in order to map onto Christendom newly conceived forms of universalism. Hermeneutically, these clerics began to imagine Jews as the irrational effect of their rationalizing programs. For Langmuir, the transformations over the twelfth century mark a move from anti-Judaism to antisemitism, that is, from epistemological to ontological categories. Abulafia, who views her work as a critical extension and also a significant rethinking of Langmuir, avoids such binaries. Her analysis comes close to conceiving the problem as one of repetition, although she does not articulate that process explicitly. Jeremy Cohen, in an elaboration of his earlier study *The Friars and the Jews: The Evolution of Medieval Anti-Judaism* (1982), and in dialogue with the work of Amos Funkenstein's *Perceptions of Jewish History*, traces the hermeneutic history of the textualized Jew in theological discourses and also detects a turning point in twelfth-century treatises. As Christian clerics subsequently mobilized their imperfect (at best) knowledge of the Talmud, they claimed that the Talmud disqualified medieval Jews as faithful witnesses to the Hebrew Scriptures. "Talmud" Jews could not be regarded as biblical Jews. Therefore, they argued that the Augustinian contract, which protected Jews as witnesses of the incomplete nature of redemption, need not be extended to such false "Talmud Jews," as medieval Jews came to be imagined.[11]

In spite of their different emphases, the narratives of Langmuir, Abulafia, and Cohen converge with Moore's timing of a significant downturn in medieval Jewish-Christian relations. They diverge mostly in their rhetorical ambivalence about explicitly labeling such transformation over the twelfth century as "antisemitic" (Langmuir), or as a radically deepened, more virulent form of "anti-Jewish" intolerance (Abulafia, Cohen, and also Gilbert Dahan). What is of interest to my argument is how their ambivalent struggles rehearse the very indeterminateness of typological thinking: does ontology supersede epistemology; does antisemitism supersede anti-Judaism? The anxious strategies to periodize or not to periodize Jewish-Christian relations are, I argue, an anxiety about the supersessionary fantasy at the core of the typological imaginary. Julia Lupton reminds us of its pervasive effect on historical periodization: typological thinking, she writes, is one of the "foundational principles of modern periodization per se, and thus must be dialectically engaged rather than simply rejected or replaced."[12]

A younger generation of medieval scholars, writing in the mid-1990s, turned to local studies as a way of questioning Moore's thesis.[13] David Nirenberg, in his award-winning book *Communities of Violence*, takes Moore to task for constructing a "structural" tale of antisemitism cast as a teleological inevitability rooted in the collective European unconsciousness. He seeks to refute "the widespread notion that we can best understand intolerance by stressing the fundamental continuity between collective systems of thought across historical time." To counteract such teleology, he advocates the study of historical agency. Agency for Nirenberg is an ontological category, meaning that it grounds the "local" and thus enables Nirenberg to assume the local as an empirical given of geography and not as a cultural construct. The local forms the backdrop for his study of how Christians, Jews, and Muslims engaged in processes of barter and negotiation and how their choices shaped the local relations of violence and tolerance. He carefully circumscribes his research synchronically and thus does not analyze the reasons why relations did change and murderously so. So constructed, his study paradoxically produces its own ahistorical category, that of agency, analogous to the ahistorical category of antisemitism of which he accuses Moore and other so-called structuralists. What if both historic agency and local context are, indeed, discursive (then and now) and therefore subject to the binding of fantasy? How does leaving untouched the unhistoricity of fantasy trouble the arguments of both Moore and Nirenberg?

Miri Rubin is also very cautious about the Moore thesis in her discussion of the vicissitudes of host desecration narratives. She, too, foregrounds agency, context, and choice, but also implies a story of periodization not dissimilar to those of Moore and Cohen. The host desecration narrative, according to Rubin, is a "new" story that emerges over the later twelfth and thirteenth centuries and marks a transformation in how Christians came to regard the mission of the Jews. Their witness was no longer one of reminder of the incompleteness of redemption, but rather "of witness [that] was worked through his [the Jew's] death, the erasure of the doubt and danger he represented." Thus, murderous Christian narratives directed against Jews gain momentum through dissemination of these stories and their visual representation. The occasions when Christians chose not to act on such fantasies provide Rubin with her rare but redemptive proof that antisemitism is not historically essential or teleological. Choice functions for Rubin, too, as the ontological given of the historical subject. The repetitive pressures that fantasy exerted on agency at the visual and narrative edges of host desecration stories remain an unconsidered question in *Gentile Narratives*.

Perhaps the most ambivalent of the recent studies is that by Sara Lipton—*Images of Intolerance: The Representation of Jews and Judaism in the Bible moralisée*.[14] Her study of the powerful and disturbing depiction of Jews in these manuscripts of the early thirteenth century argues with Moore over the level of consciousness ascribed to such portrayals. On one page Lipton faults Moore for imputing too much consciousness to clerical elites in the process of producing denigrating stereotypes of Jews; on the next, she remarks that he has imputed too little consciousness to this process. Her careful construction of the provenance of these manuscripts also raises the question of agency. Lipton begins to acknowledge the discursive possibilities of agency when she observes that "the resonances of the new semantic practices were not always confined to the illustrated page or the spoken word."

These recent studies are persuasive in their questioning of an ahistorical notion of antisemitism as a way of understanding the history of Jewish-Christian relations. At the same time, they also show the limits of relying on ontological notions of historical agency without considering fantasy and pleasure. My own study seeks to embrace the paradox of material network and fantasy. What follows does rely on psychoanalysis, not for the purpose of reintroducing some timeless notion of antisemitism, but to interrogate psychoanalytic thinking, too, for its own investments in the typological imaginary, even as psychoanalytic theory offers us ways of imagining new ways of relating, or what Eric Santner has called an ethics of singularity. My study is thus a percussive one in that it seeks to loosen the sediments and accretions of rigid fantasies that hold "Christian-ness" captive.

Mise-en-Page and the Foreskin

The crucial point of all this so far is that figural or typological thinking has at its core a fantasy of supersession that historians need to work through in order to transform the way we think about Jewish-Christian relations then and now. This book takes the typological imaginary as its central problem. It does so, however, not through the means of already well-studied texts of medieval exegesis and polemic against the Jews. Instead, I focus on the machine-like repetitions, the automaticity at the typological core of the Christian unconscious. From the moment in his epistles that he transferred the cut of circumcision to an inscription on the heart, Paul constituted typological thinking with and through graphic technologies with their attendant questions of legibility. In his new theology of circumcision, the circumcision of the heart, Paul severed a Christian "now" from a Jewish "then." As he wrote in Romans 2: 28–29, "For he is not a Jew, which is one outwardly; neither is that circumcision which is outward in the flesh: But he is a Jew, which is one inwardly; and circumcision is that of the heart, in the spirit, and not in the letter; whose praise not of men but of God."

Typology and graphic technology are thus closely bound, and, I shall argue, historically constitutive of each other. There exists, however, no history of their imbrication. Such a history would be one precondition for working through the Christian fantasy of supersession. In advocating the transfer of circumcision from the cut foreskin to the inscribed heart, Paul incorporated fleshly excision into a space of inscription. In fabricating the heart as a space of inscription, Paul also inaugurated the typologization of the graphic machine, in that the act of cutting the foreskin becomes the figure for Christian inscription, or graphic technologies. Graphic technologies are thus the chief evidentiary source of my study.

Let me now exemplify what I mean by graphic technologies by returning us to the page of the *Glossa ordinaria* that opened this introduction. The standardized layout of the page illustrated in Figure 1 marked a major transition in Christian graphic technology in the mid-twelfth century. The concept of the page as a modular unit for the graphic organization of textual presentation emerged at that time as scribes and scholars devised a standardized layout for this schoolbook. No component of these textbooks—the Bible text, the interlinear gloss, or the marginal glosses—was itself an innovation. Indeed, each element has a complicated genealogy in early medieval biblical scholarship. What interests me for my study of the typological imaginary is how the page fabricated as a modular unit came to organize Bible text and glosses graphically and subordinate them to itself.

Christopher de Hamel has carefully analyzed the crucial scribal experiments involved in producing the standardized, modular form for the pages of the *Glossa*.[15] Whereas once the Bible text had been the chief organizing vector for scribes, who wrote the text out first and, then, organized the glossing around it, scribes in the mid-twelfth century began to conceive of the page as the unit of graphic organization. We can observe them laying out each page first according to a repetitive rationalized grid of lines and margins by pricking and ruling parchment from margin to margin, leaf after leaf. The Bible text itself no longer determined the scribal vicissitudes of the page. Instead, the repetitive mise-en-page graphically organized the inscription of text and commentaries: "Sometime after the middle of the twelfth century, apparently in the 1160s, a complete change occurred in the layout of northern French glossed books. The ruling was drawn closer together and was written right across the written area" (24). For each page these formal graphic changes produced an exemplary text of forty lines of gloss in the left and right hand margins with twenty lines of biblical text written on alternate lines in the center. Scribes wrote the interlinear gloss between the lines of the central biblical text.[16] As Ivan Illich has observed (and as Figure 1 from a printed *Glossa ordinaria* depicts): "the textual patterning of the book page had such a strong hold on the imagination that Gutenberg and his pupils did what they could to make its essentials survive into the age of print."[17] Not surprisingly, as the page was transformed graphically so was the concept of the Bible as book transformed materially. According to de Hamel, by the second half of the twelfth century owners came to think of glossed books of the Bible not as a collection, or assemblage, of books, but as a corpus, albeit in multivolume form. The Bible thus came to be imagined as a sequenced entity.[18] The changing material notions of the Bible as a bookish artifact could only intensify typological operations.[19]

The fabrication of the page as a modular unit by means of a repetitive, graphic process (the pricking and uniform ruling across the surface of the page) transformed typological thinking from within. The interface, the page, and the fantasy, the typological imaginary, shared the graphic technology of ruling and repetition. As we have already observed, the interlinear gloss juxtaposed the names of New Testament fulfillment onto the names of the figures of the Old Testament text. The graphic organization worked as a *visual* as well as a *rhetorical* mode of substitution. The modular framework of a unified and unifying page format rendered typological thinking as an image, that is, as a kind of diagram placed in the central field of the page in which the biblical text is inscribed.

It is possible to imagine the newly conceived interface, the mise-en-page in the *Glossa ordinaria*, as a little machine. Precisely and repetitiously it rotates the littera back onto the figura and begins to produce typological effects mechanically at the level of the graphic. The rhetoric of typology is subjected to the mechanicity of a graphic form. The layout of the glossed Bible rationalizes textual organization and thus renders typology, once an argument about reference, now also a representation. The modular page works as a kind of typological viewing device: anticipating the device illustrated by Dürer, in which the artist draws a female nude by looking through a transparent screen squared by threads that correspond to the gridded page on which he is drawing.[20] Analogously the biblical scholar views the Old Testament through the viewing device of the new mise-en-page, which enables him to map the typological imaginary onto the Old Testament.

Within a quarter century of the stabilized graphic form of the *Glossa*, we find the central space of such pricked and ruled pages "built over" by an elaborate and disturbingly innovative illustrative program in manuscripts that have been dubbed *Bibles moralisées*. This genre evacuated the Bible text and in its emptied central space substituted a new graphic program of illuminated roundels. Sara Lipton has exhaustively studied the earliest illustrated examples of the *Bible moralisée* (Vienna, ÖNB 2554; Vienna, ÖNB 1179).[21] These two luxury manuscripts were produced in Capetian court circles between 1208 and the 1220, over a period marked by important royal and papal legislation about Jews as well as the incorporation of the university at Paris.[22] Their visual program is obsessed with Jews, who are depicted in 39.7 percent of the roundels and are mentioned by name in 15.7 percent of the adjacent commentary texts. The painstaking research of John Lowden has shown how their designers, like those scribes of the *Glossa ordinaria*, regarded the page as a unit. The eight medallions, which occupy the central area designed for the biblical text in the *Glossa ordinaria*, were planned and illuminated before the addition of biblical text and moralizing commentary in the right and left margins. In a comparison of biblical text and commentary for the Book of Ruth in seven extant *Bibles moralisées*, Lowden has shown that the biblical passages, paraphrases, show an "undergraduate" knowledge of the Bible and that most of its moralizing paraphrases depart from the textbook version of the *Glossa ordinaria*.[23]

My chief concern is with the formal graphic level exemplified by folio 3v, taken from the purportedly earliest version of the *Bible moralisée* (Vienna, ÖNB 2554) and reproduced in Figure 2. The commentary, translated from the medieval French by Gerald Guest, reads as follows:

3vA
Here Noah plants his vine and drinks the wine from which he gets drunk (Gen 9: 20–21).

3va
That Noah planted the vine and drank the wine, which he himself planted, signifies Jesus Christ, who planted the Jews and drank from the wine at the Passion.

3vB
Here Noah sleeps, and one of his children uncovers him, and the others are ashamed and cover him (Gen 9: 21–23).

3vb
That one of the brothers uncovered him and the others cover him signifies the Jews who uncovered the shame of Jesus Christ and the Christians who covered him.

3vC
Here the pagans make the Tower of Babel, against the commandment of God, and God strikes them down and turns their work to nothing (Gen 11: 4–9).

3vc
That the pagans began the tower of Babel against God's commandment signifies the astronomers and the dialecticians who make false proofs against the will of Jesus Christ, and He turns their work to nothing and blinds them and strikes them.

3vD
Here the pagans come and throw Abraham and another into the fire, and God saves Abraham because of his good faith, and the other was put back and was burned.

3vd
That Abraham was in the fire and God saved him because of his good faith signifies those who are in the fire of the world, in covetousness

and lust, and God saves them because of their strong faith, and he who was put back signifies those who remain in mortal sin and are burned.

The lining and pricking of the page is readily visible and the reader can see that the illuminations are the first layer to be laid down over

Figure 2. *Bible moralisée*, Vienna, ÖNB 2554. By permission of Österreichische Nationalbibliotek Vienna.

the gridded page. Scribes inserted the commentary at a later stage in the graphic process. The concatenation of roundels relies on the alteration and repetition of interlinear gloss and Bible text already familiar from the *Glossa ordinaria* (which textbook was familiar to the designers of the *Bible moralisée*). I have chosen this particular folio page to consider at greater length because it contains the first mention of Abraham, who indexes the covenant of circumcision, even though the *Bible moralisée* skips over Genesis 17 and any direct reference to the covenant between God and Abraham. The specter of covenant anxiously haunts the composition of folio 3v, especially in the concerns about genital uncovering and the same and "new" knowledge foregrounded there. Roundel 3vB depicts the story of the sons of Noah, one of whom uncovers the genitals of Noah as he sleeps in a drunken stupor. His brothers, who feel ashamed at the sight, cover him. This story is then glossed by roundel 3vb, which depicts a scene in which Jews are unwinding the loincloth of the crucified Christ. They point at what they have exposed. The commentary to this roundel shifts the key of shame. In the roundel above, it was the two sons of Noah who were ashamed. In the lower roundel it is the "shame of Jesus" that the Jews see and the Christians cover. This shame or scandal that the Jews are scrutinizing is the circumcised penis of Christ. This scandalous knowledge of the cut of the foreskin is transposed in the lower roundel (3vC), which links the destruction of the Tower of Babel with folio 3vc, in which Jesus smites the emergent "university" men of the twelfth century, the dialecticians and the astronomers. The ensemble of roundels enables the scaling up and down of questions of shame from the register of sexual knowledge to learned knowledge. Most important, as Sara Lipton has already compellingly argued, the visual and textual commentary cut off and cut out contemporary Jews from their relationship to the Old Law.

What has transpired graphically in these "moralized Bibles" resonates with observations made by Walter Benjamin in his study of later baroque allegory. He noted the tendency for allegorical writing to become visual and for history to become part of its setting or script. When this happened, he argued, history becomes a ruin.[24] I think we can find a prehistory of this repetitive baroque process as the *Glossa ordinaria* mutated into moralized Bibles. The graphic machine of the mise-en-page rendered ruinous the Bible verses that occupied the central area of the glossed page. Not surprisingly, we find this ruined space invaded by the extensive visual programs of the *Bibles moralisées*. They mistake stereotype for typology. In other words in the twelfth century, typology, as a supersessionary epistemological process, becomes a graphic stereotype. Should we then interpret this new

graphic operation just described as yet another example of the intensification of anti-Judaic feelings of the kind detected by medieval
scholars who have studied theological polemic of the twelfth century?

This book poses anew the very terms of the question. It explores
how graphics repetitiously enact the cut of the foreskin at the same
time that graphic processes insist on the legibility of the circumcision
of the heart. The collision of cutting and inscribing takes place not
only in the rhetorical realm of identification (and therefore desire for
self and other), where inclusion or exclusion is at stake, but also in
the insistent realm of the mechanical, arbitrary in its principle. Such
graphic mechanicity repeatedly reminds us that the foreskin is the disturbing remnant at the heart of Christian typology. Cutting into the
surface of the page with pricking and ruling is in fact a repetitious
graphic effort to ground Christian typology. The graphic technologies provide media through which fantasies organize the pleasures of
the Christian typological imaginary.

I attempt to intervene in the typological imaginary in order to
reopen this gap between typology and inscription once collapsed by
Paul. Repetitions are the clues that I track. Chapter 1 shows how
graphic technologies, in the form of scientific diagrams, begin to
insinuate themselves even into polemical tracts in the twelfth century.
I study how the scientific diagrams that interrupted the text of the
widely disseminated polemic of Petrus Alfonsi cut graphic boundaries
between Christian reason and Jewish unreason. These borders of reason and unreason also come to be drawn graphically on contemporary *mappaemundi*. Such realms of unreason do not disappear in the
chastened spaces of the purportedly more scientific maps of the Ptolemaic tradition printed in the later fifteenth century. A careful study of
the ways in which early printers exploited the modular mise-en-page
to develop front matter (indexes) and back matter (re-presentation of
medieval "marvels" literature) for their editions of Ptolemy actually
links them with the medieval graphic tradition of *mappaemundi*. The
repetition of such graphic projects graphed Jewish stereotypes in the
always already failed project of materializing the foreskin that Christian supersession graphically supersedes.

In Chapter 2 I take up the well-established textbook genre of the
medieval universal history. These histories conceived temporality in
terms of six or seven ages of salvation history and used the holy city
of Jerusalem as a kind of navel that bound together the vision of temporality. I show how the mechanicity of printing the well-established
genre of medieval universal histories broke up and rendered incoher-
ent the carefully delineated time lines used to illustrate universal histories. The graphic organization of the *Nuremberg Chronicle*, printed in

1493, exemplifies this process. I examine how the dissemination of so-called "realistic" city views in printed versions of universal history increasingly fragmented the time lines. By the time of the publication of the grandiose *Chronicle,* even Jerusalem, the "navel" of the universal history, had been excised from its customary central and binding place in the genre. Once Jerusalem had been cut out, supersessionary fantasies reorganized identifications both among Christians and between Christians and Jews. Out of the exploded temporality of the universal history falls graphic debris in the form of repeatedly featured woodcuts of fetishized historical synagogue furniture and aggressive renditions of "Talmud" Jews being burned to death in pogroms.

The third chapter takes up the problems of Christian graphic technologies at the level of the archive and architectural space. It relates an exemplary reading of Albrecht Altdorfer's 1519 etching of the interior of the synagogue at Regensburg, drawn just before its destruction, to the famous trial of Baruch the Jew transcribed in Bishop Fournier's trial register (1320). The carefully regulated transcripts of inquisitorial trials (their graphic supplement) expressed a graphic crisis regarding the *legibility* of baptism as the circumcision of the heart. Christians framed their anxieties in terms of questions about the sacramental efficacy of baptism for Jews.[25] How could inquisitors "read" the converted, baptized hearts of circumcised Jews?[26] The trial transcripts provided ways of forging further links in the chain of graphic repetition, thus disseminating the fantasy of graphic efficacy. The chapter raises questions about the aggressive and paradoxical Christian use of graphics to erase Jewish communities temporally in a fantasy-ridden effort to have them materialize as typological matter. It also shows that Christians not only sought to reoccupy the community space of the Jews that they had destroyed, but that they also sought to occupy that space metaphorically through graphic repetition. This is the graphic story of a Christian hermeneutic circle—how the *corpus mysticum* (the church on earth) becomes the *fidelis synagoga* (faithful synagogue). The chapter concludes, perhaps unexpectedly, with Foucault. It ponders how his efforts to rethink temporality and history foundered on the typological imaginary and uses that foundering as a way, once again, to intervene in the typological imaginary.

Typology never lets go; its repetitions, as I have already suggested, haunt some psychoanalytic approaches as well as compelling postcolonial histories that are attempting to rethink temporality without supersession in its theological or secular modalities. In Chapters 4 and 5 I return to the foreskin, the fantasized remnant of the Christian typological imaginary, in order to question the Lacanian argument that there can be no "pre-modern" uncanny. What supersessionary fantasies are at stake in the Lacanian claim that the uncanny is only constitutive of the modern? I argue that these Lacanian arguments mistake the uncanny for the foreskin. They cannot think that within the phallus there lodges the temporal kernel of the circumcised foreskin, of a temporality which is not one. I argue that the foreskin is the "unhistorical" (not ahistorical) remainder of the uncanny that is the unassimilable temporality that exceeds their Lacanian periodization of the uncanny. Chapter 4 opens with a discussion of the recent debate over lachrymose history in medieval studies. In 1928, Salo Wittmayer Baron, the first scholar to hold an academic chair in Jewish history and culture, labeled those nineteenth-century studies by Jewish scholars, which emphasized the desolate history of persecution of medieval Jews, as misleading "lachrymose history" or "Jammergeschichte," his more abjecting designation of such history. Subsequently a younger generation of post-Holocaust medieval scholars has taken up his crusade against lachrymose history because of its perceived tendency to render antisemitism as some inevitable, ahistoric aspect of the Christian unconscious. This chapter on lachrymose history looks into the unconscious of lachrymose history in two ways. First, it examines the history of repressing medieval Ashkenazi lamentation in the Reform liturgy crafted by Jewish scholars of the Wissenschaft des Judentums. It then reads *Moses and Monotheism* (a belated text of that movement) for the return of repressed lamentation through the history of circumcision recounted by Sigmund Freud. I read *Moses and Monotheism,* in which Freud designates circumcision as "uncanny," through his well-known essay on the uncanny published two decades earlier. My reading of Freud shows that circumcision poses the question of a temporality that is not one and that the historicist appeal to periodization cannot answer such a question. Indeed, typology's work is to deny the very existence of such a question even as it repetitiously seeks to materialize the foreskin. Chapter 5 examines how the supersessionary afterlife of graphic excision of the Jews haunts sophisticated postcolonial efforts to rethink historiographical periodization. In an acclaimed postcolonial ethnography, *In an Antique Land,* by Amitav Ghosh, I study the surfacing of circumcision as a problem in the text which returns my study once again to the challenges of working through the fantasy of supersession even in postcolonial studies.

Chapter 1
Christians Mapping Jews: Cartography, Temporality, and the Typological Imaginary

> It is the sorting out that makes the times, not the times that make the sorting.
>
> —Bruno Latour

In a cogent essay critical of the ways in which "rationality" has become a mantra for dividing the pre-modern from the modern, Brian Stock has shown how the desire to push the boundaries of modernity either back to the Middle Ages, a modernizing tendency, or forward to later times, a medievalizing tendency, leaves untouched the multiple and syncopated linkages between rationality and its technologies—scientific instrumentation, textuality and subjectivity.[1] Bruno Latour takes Stock's critique even further, claiming that periodization itself is the problem of the modern.[2] Using Boyle's vacuum pump as an example, Latour shows how this "invention" can be considered as modern and revolutionary only if one starts periodizing—for example, by including certain events on a time line and excluding others (such as magic and religion) that would derail the invention's teleology.[3] Thus does Latour conclude that "time is not a general framework but a provisional result of the connection among entities."[4]

In effect, Stock and Latour both work to derationalize rationality, thereby opening up possibilities for cultural studies of its technologies and drawing our attention, not to the question of power and rationality, but to the political power *of* rationality.[5] How does "rationality" intervene to re-draw, to "re-cognize," what counts as knowledge? Stock and Latour's respective work is especially useful for interrogating medieval epistemologies, and has inspired my own interest in the tension between so-called traditional practices of medieval cartography—specifically, *mappaemundi*, the ubiquitous cartographic representation from the twelfth to the fifteenth centuries—and purportedly rational and "modern" Ptolemaic cartographic practices, which became dominant in Western Europe in the fifteenth century and were notable for locating and representing objects in gridded space. The current textbook narrative of medieval cartography typifies this tension. Although such narratives are quite sophisticated and in fact eschew any notion of linear progression in medieval mapping, they nevertheless keep separate medieval *mappaemundi* from Ptolemaic maps: "whereas the didactic and symbolic *mappaemundi* served to present the faithful with moralized versions of Christian history from the Creation to the Last Judgment, Claudius Ptolemy's instructions on how to compile a map of the known world were strictly practical."[6] Typically, the literature on medieval maps regards *mappaemundi* as encyclopedic, "unscientific," whereas Ptolemaic cartography is considered a first step toward a "modern" practice. *Mappaemundi* get sorted out as "traditional" and Ptolemaic maps as "rational." Supersession is at stake here.

This chapter attends to graphic details of these maps to tell a different story. Instead of sorting them out, it superimposes the "messy," monster-infested, encyclopedic medieval *mappaemundi* on the gridded Ptolemaic maps. Indeed, as I show, the overlaps and misalignments of these two cartographic practices graph the Christian typological imaginary in ways that need to be better understood in medieval cartography in particular and medieval studies in general.[7] To explain what is at stake in viewing the *relationship* between these cartographic practices as I do, I turn briefly to the work of anthropologist Johannes Fabian, who has studied early modern ethnography (a mapping practice in its own right) and its constructions of time and the other. Fabian claims that early modern ethnography came to deny what he calls the "coevalness," or contemporaneity, of its encounter with the other. According to Fabian, such denial occurs when there is a "persistent and systematic tendency to place the referent(s) of anthropology in a Time other than the present of the producer of anthropological discourse."[8] In other words, rather than seeing itself as coeval with its referent, or part of the same time, anthropology tended instead to deny this coevalness and imagine itself as part of an allegedly more modern and rational time, and its referent part of a more primitive, irrational time.

Early modern ethnography did not, however, initiate such practices. When early Christians cut off Jews and their Hebrew scriptures from the "now" and placed them in a past superseded by the New Testament, they inaugurated the denial of coevalness. This chapter traces how the Christian typological imaginary extended itself to cartographic practices. Medieval maps helped to fabricate contemporary Jews as the first ethnographic "primitives," since, as I shall show, medieval mapping practices denied coevalness to Jews, just as social scientists rendered primitive their anthropological "referents." To rephrase Fabian and draw on the work of Jonathan Boyarin, there is a "persistent and systematic tendency" to place Jews in a time other than the supersessionary present of Christendom.

What follows is an attempt to delineate some of the ways medieval Christians used graphic technologies to inscribe supersession cartographically. Medieval maps became an important graphic surface for the Christian typological imaginary. Cartographic inscription was neither neutral nor insignificant, for, as we shall see, translating Jews from time into space was a way in which medieval Christians could colonize—by imagining that they exercised dominion over supersession.[9] Although one of the goals of this chapter is to bring the typological imaginary of medieval mapping practices into view, medieval maps cannot be thought about in isolation, since the very notion of a map as an isolated stand-alone object is already an effect of modernist production of cartographic space. Both *mappaemundi* and Ptolemaic maps need to be studied as links in a chain of translations that graphically dispossessed medieval Jews of coevalness. This chapter, therefore, reads maps within a *network* of translations in order to discern their interacting imaginaries. The network includes diverse but relevant textual material, such as twelfth-century anti-Jewish polemic, fourteenth-century travel literature, and fifteenth-century Christian-Hebrew studies, as well as the instruments of translation, namely, astrolabes and alphabets.

The "Mother" of the Astrolabe: Dispossessing the Foreskin

I start with the dispossessions that take place in the most widely disseminated of medieval anti-Jewish polemics, Petrus Alfonsi's *Dialogue Against the Jews* (1108–1110). In this *Dialogue*, Petrus Alfonsi, himself a converted Jew, educated in Arabic, learned in biblical Hebrew, an ambassador of Arabic science to France and England, disputes with his former Jewish self, which he enfolds in the persona of his interlocutor called Moses. He wields his *Dialogue* like a knife to excise this former self.[10] His polemic is distinctive for deploying not only scientific arguments, but also, for the first time in this genre, scientific diagrams. He uses "science" to discredit talmudic knowledge for its irrationality.[11] In the *Dialogue*'s longest scientific excursus, Alfonsi attacks the talmudic exegesis of Nehemiah 9: 6, "the hosts of heaven shall worship thee," which locates the dwelling of God in the West. Only rabbinical ignorance of the concepts of time and longitude, according to Alfonsi, could allow such error to persist. After unveiling Moses' ignorance, he then proceeds to teach him an astronomy lesson wherein he asserts the relativity of East and West, of dawn and sunset. Alfonsi's astronomy lesson teaches the concept of longitude, whereby the contingent position of the observer using an astrolabe to take measurements determines relative timing and spacing. By marking such a difference between talmudic interpretation and the instrumentality of astronomy, Alfonsi implicitly constructs the rational observer as a Christian (male) and excludes Jews from this privileged position, the site of the one who knows. Alfonsi thus uses the "reason" of science in this excursus to deny his coevalness with Moses and to relegate him to a time other than the present of his scientific discourse. Science trumps or supersedes the Talmud.

The astronomy lesson of the *Dialogue* drew on knowledge of the astrolabe.[12] Astronomy texts and astrolabes dating from the eleventh and twelfth centuries document Jewish and Arabic use of the astrolabe in Andalusian Spain.[13] Of the six Andalusian astrolabes surviving from the eleventh century, one of the oldest, dated to 1029–30 from its inscription, has scratched on its surface the Hebrew equivalents for certain engraved Arabic star-names (Figure 3a, b). These graffiti attest to the cross-cultural use of this instrument. Scientific texts also indicate active Jewish participation in astronomical and astrological studies at Andalusian courts in the early twelfth century. A Toledan Jew, Abraham ibn Ezra, wrote eight noted treatises in astrology, among which is his treatise on the astrolabe (1146–48). The earliest set of astronomical tables in Hebrew, drawn up by Abraham Bar Hiyya in 1104, just predates the conversion of Petrus Alfonsi. The *Dialogue* thus misrepresents the actual technological expertise of contemporary Jews and in so doing dispossesses them of their own astrolabes as well as their scientific texts.[14]

This historical evidence for such close intertwining of Arabic and Jewish astronomical studies and instruments makes Alfonsi's dispossession of Jews from astronomical discourse all the more stunning. Alfonsi stripped Jews of their coeval contribution to Andalusian astronomy and then infantilized and feminized their talmudic learning as the "verba jocantium in scholis puerorum, vel nentium in plateis mulierum" ("joking words of schoolboys and gossip of women in the streets").[15] Alfonsi could imagine the "universal" rational principles of the astrolabe as a means to purify him of his "pre-conversion"

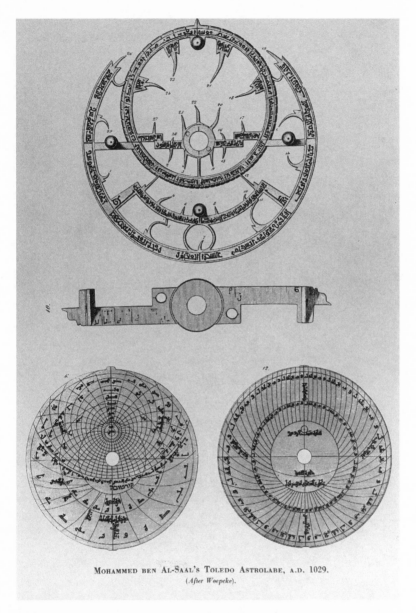

MOHAMMED BEN AL-SAAL'S TOLEDO ASTROLABE, A.D. 1029.
(After Woepcke).

Figure 3a. Andalusian astrolabe by Mohammed ben Al-Saal, 1029. As reproduced in Robert T. Gunther, *The Eastern Astrolabes*, vol. 1 of *Astrolabes of the World*, 3rd ed. (London: William Holland Press, 1972), no. 116.

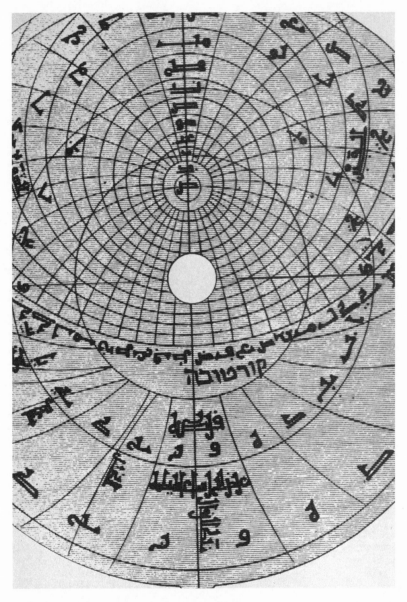

Figure 3b. Detail of the Hebrew equivalent of the engraved Arabic star names on Mohammed ben Al-Saal's 1029 astrolabe.

self, of the talmudic Jew, whom he abjects in the *Dialogue.* Since the
astrolabe relativizes time by linking it to the circuits of the sun and
stars, Petrus Alfonsi, with astrolabe in hand, need no longer remain
incarnated temporally, ontologically, in that abject place from which
Moses is said to come in the *Dialogue.* Alfonsi literally diagrams for
himself a new place in the sun. The astrolabe thus becomes the instru-
mental means by which Alfonsi can both dispossess himself of his former Jewish self and through its possession ward off the shattering
aspects of the dispossession he effects; in a word, the astrolabe is, for
Alfonsi, a fetish.[16]

Theological Telephones

At the very time Alfonsi was writing his anti-Jewish polemic, Christian
biblical scholars of the Victorine school in Paris engaged local Jewish
intellectuals in ways that Beryl Smalley and her students have thought
of as cooperative, respectful, curious. Could it be that the Victorine
interaction with local Jewish intellectuals fostered a sense of coevalness that might counteract Alfonsi's denial to his Jewish interlocutor?
These same Victorines knew Alfonsi's *Dialogue.* In eight instances of
the sixty-eight manuscripts in which the *Dialogue* was bound together
with other texts, it traveled with Victorine texts. Two volumes of the
Alfonsi text were also to be found in their Paris library. Thus the Victorines could consult local rabbis and read anti-Jewish polemic at the
same time. To explore this paradox, I investigated the dissemination
of cartographic interests among the Victorines. The early twelfth century marks a turning point for the production of *mappaemundi.* An
important text, *Imago mundi,* written in 1110 by Honorius Augustodunensis, precipitated renewed interest in maps. His cosmography
treated celestial and terrestrial geography, the measurement of time,
and the six ages of universal history.[17] Largely conservative and deeply
derivative, its simplicity and clarity nevertheless guaranteed its wide
circulation and broad influence. During the twelfth century Honorius's text can be found traveling bound with Hugh of St. Victor's *De
Arca Noe* (1128–29) as well as with Petrus Alfonsi's *Dialogue Against the
Jews.* The library of St. Victor possessed two copies of this *Imago mundi,*
and, when Hugh of St. Victor wrote his *Descriptio mappe mundi* in 1128
or 1129, he drew on Honorius's treatise.

Victorines promoted the fabrication and study of maps. Knowledge
of place-names and locations was crucial to Victorine innovations in
biblical exegesis. The cartographic texts and maps they introduced
into their schoolrooms also inspired their meditations on temporality
and history. Hugh of St. Victor viewed history as a narrative sequence,

a *series narrationis*: "if we investigate things carefully according to the sequence of time, the succession of generations and the arrangement of truths taught, we can claim confidently to have reached all leaves of divine scripture."[18] He desired that this temporal "sorting out" be drawn graphically (*depingere*), because things cannot show themselves without such aids ("res ipsas non possunt presentare").[19] His insistence on representing the "visibility" of *series narrationis* through graphic media thus marks a fresh direction in the *mappaemundi* tradition. What once functioned pedagogically came to be joined among the Victorines to emerging theological notions of the visible and sacramental—that is, *mappaemundi* could now be deployed as a graphic technology of the visible, not unlike the sacraments themselves, especially the Eucharist.[20]

To refine their literal studies of the Bible, Hugh of St. Victor and his students consulted with Jewish rabbis about Hebrew philology and interpretation. In effect they approached local rabbis as intimate artifacts of the Old Testament. The question of their coevalness was a vexed one—in Beryl Smalley's compelling words: "the Jew appealed to him [the student of the Bible] as a kind of telephone to the Old Testament."[21] Like the astrolabe, the theological telephone, another technological device, paradoxically interrupted coevalness between Christian and Jewish scholars in the early twelfth century. A consideration of Victorine mapping of Jews in their apocalyptic thought can help us understand the fantasy of supersession that is intrinsic to such intellectual exchanges, in which contemporary Jews were called upon to perform as relics.

Literal readings of the Bible among Victorines not only inspired their interest in history, geography, and maps but also prompted apocalyptic speculations. The apocalyptic mapping of the enclosed peoples of Gog and Magog onto *mappaemundi* can help to track ways in which such maps troubled the coevalness of Jews. Pedagogical texts such as Hugh's *Descriptio* are a case in point.[22] Early patristic, rabbinical, and Qur'anic scholars speculated on the identity of Gog and Magog. To this commentary attached different versions of the enclosure of peoples and their eruption as a sign of the Last Days. Not mapped as a locus on late Roman maps from which prototypes of the *mappaemundi* borrowed, nor for that matter depicted on the early *mappaemundi* of the Beatus Apocalypse group, Gog and Magog begin to appear as entries on twelfth-century maps drawn under the influence of Victorine biblical studies.[23] Increasingly over the twelfth-century, texts and maps link the Jews with stories of the enclosed peoples of Gog and Magog. As early as Orosius in the fifth century, links in this chain of associations of Gog and Magog with the Jews begin to be forged. He attached to the story of the birth of Alexander the Great, builder of Alexander's Gate to enclose Gog and Magog, a tale of the deportation of Jews to the area of the Gate from which they will eventually erupt in the last days.[24] Importantly, in his *Descriptio,* Hugh of St. Victor textually maps Gog and Magog with the apocalyptic tradition: "contra has regiones, in oceano septrionali, sunt insule in quibus habitant gentes ille Gog Magog, de quibus in Apocalypsi legitur" ("abutting this region, in the western ocean are islands in which live that people, Gog Magog, about which it is written in the Apocalypse").[25] In his widely disseminated canonical encyclopedia of biblical history, *Historia scholastica,* Peter Comestor (d. 1179), a member of the Victorine circle who retired to St. Victor in his last years, further forged the links in the chain between apocalypse, Gog and Magog, and Jews by specifically identifying the ten lost tribes of Israel as the peoples enclosed behind Alexander's Gate.[26] Victorines thus inscribed Jews on *mappaemundi* when they marked the site of Gog and Magog.

Herein lies the paradox of Victorines consulting with local Jews at the same time that they graphed Jews into the insurrections of the Last Days. The apocalyptic telos of the Victorines envisioned the apocalypse as a radical space stripped of earthly time. The combination of long distance telephone calls to the Old Testament made by Victorines via Parisian Jews, in tandem with their locating Jews as the enclosed peoples of the apocalyptic Gog and Magog, thus had the effect of a double detemporalization. It robbed these Jews of a *past* in the present by dispossessing them of their coeval engagement with science and hermeneutics in the medieval world. Moreover this apocalyptic scripting deprived them of a *future* in the present, that is, an open-ended, contingent, "history that will be."[27] To understand the deepening process of dispossession, I now turn to the problem of graphic inscription itself.

Graphic Dispossession: "For I had lettres"

The astrolabe, depictions of Gog and Magog, and attitudes toward contemporary medieval Jews converge in the *Travels of Mandeville,* a popular travel book of the later fourteenth century.[28] The *Travels* further overlays such convergence with maps of different alphabets that punctuate the text. The Hebrew alphabet comes to be marked as a tool of threat and conspiracy against Christians.[29] The *Travels,* like the work of the Victorine school, has, nevertheless, been praised by scholars such as Mary Campbell and Stephen Greenblatt for its tolerance. Yet the Jews, Greenblatt notes, were the "most significant exception

to tolerance."[30] The force of their exclusion strikes even more when
the model of human diversity in the *Travels* is taken into account.
Drawing on prevalent astrological notions regarding the influence
of the movement of the stars and planets on human nature, the *Travels* argues that it is not "who" you were (identity), but "where" you
were (geography) that accounted for human diversity. The reliance
on contingency of place instead of some fixed notion of human
essence did foster tolerance, until this astrological model of human
diversity intersected with an apocalyptic tradition of "astrological"
theology. It is to that tradition that I now turn briefly, since an understanding of its influence on the narrator of the *Travels* can help to
delineate how a profound dispossession of Jews rests at the heart of
this so-called tolerant astrological model of human diversity.

Throughout the fourteenth century, medieval scholars increasingly
sought to calibrate the "time line" of universal history with calculations from astronomy and astrology in order to refine predictions
for the onset of the Last Days.[31] Valerie Flint has observed that early
in the *Imago mundi* Honorius consistently interpolated information
on astrology and magic into his revisions of his world history. Pierre
d'Ailly (1350–1420), whose 1410 *Imago mundi* Christopher Columbus
read and annotated, attempted to align the relative chronologies
found in world histories (drawn from such diverse sources as biblical history, Greek and Roman history, papal lists, and the events of
contemporary history) onto an "independent" time line dated by astrological conjunctions. Students of conjunctions had studied, in particular, the "historical" paths of Saturn and Jupiter through the zodiac
and observed their relations to each other. Using their conjunctions
as chronological points, d'Ailly then constructed his astrological time
line which provided for a serial transition from past to future, from
history to prophecy. In order to authorize this "scientific" approach to
theological temporality, scholars needed to prognosticate successfully.
The ensuing pressure to predict events contributed to an overdetermining concern with timing of the advent of Antichrist: "l'astrologie
devient une herméneutique de l'apocalypse chrétienne."[32] Calculation of that advent entangled astrological theology with popular
conflations of medieval Jews with Gog and Magog, whose eruption
would be the sign of his coming.[33] Thus scholarly models of "human
diversity" paradoxically resonated with popular notions that denied
Jewish neighbors their coevalness.

The exclusion of Jews from this tolerant astrological model of
human diversity can be traced in the *Travels* through the medium of
the alphabet. What astrology liberally relativized in the *Travels*, its
alphabet-lore reinstalled as a hard line between West and East. The

Travels uses a geography of the alphabet as one of its chief ploys to exclude Jews.[34] Alphabets appear in the text when the narrator arrives at the border of a region. At that point he traces out the forms and names of the letters of its alphabet. Such topographical edges and their respective alphabets occur along Mandeville's route in the following order: Greek, Egyptian, Hebrew, Saracen, Persian, and Chaldean. This alphabetical mapping exercise ends as the traveler comes to the islands of India. At the juncture the narrative turns from a traceable land route to a watery voyage marked by the interruptions of the many islands of an archipelago.

As the *Travels* encounters Indians it waxes "rational," just as Alfonsi did in his *Dialogue* when he countered Moses and his talmudic interpretation with scientific discussion of the contingency of longitude. The traveler leaves alphabets behind on the Indian archipelago and enters a world governed by stars.[35] The longest commentary on the astral geography of the archipelago occurs on the Indian isle of Lamary where, the author informs his reader, the Lamarians live in a state of nature. They go naked and hold sexual partners and property in common. Lamarians observe no rule of descent and parcel out their offspring to sexual partners without distinctions. Since they recognize no rules of kinship and therefore have no incest taboo, it is not surprising to learn that the Larmarians are the first cannibals to be encountered in the *Travels*. They literally perform the undoing of kinship by eating their children. Christian readers, who were familiar with exempla and also ritual murder stories that portrayed Jews as the local cannibals of Christendom, certainly might think of Jews when they read about Lamarians.[36] It is precisely at this overdetermined juncture that the narrator begins his discourse on the astrolabe. He argues for the roundness of the earth and its circumnavigability by means of a lecture on longitude:[37]

The whiche thing I prove thus, after that i have seyn. For I have ben toward the partes of Braban and beholden in the Astrolabre that the steere that is clept the transmontayne is liiii. degrees high, And more forthere in Almayne and Bewme it hath lviii. degrees, and more forth toward the parties Septemtrioneles it is lxii. degrees of heghte and certeyn mynutes, for I self have mesured it be the Astrolabe.[38]

After this technological interlude, the *Travels* then leaves behind the cannibalistic Lamarians in order to pass on to the lands of Prester John. The site of Gog and Magog, however, stands directly in the way. Once again Jews interrupt the itinerary, this time not evocatively, as in the case of the Lamarians, but overtly, as the *Travels* describes the ten lost tribes enclosed in Gog and Magog.[39] According to the *Travels*

Jews cannot escape their enclosure because the only language they know is Hebrew, a language unknown to neighboring communities:

> and also thei conen no langage but only hire owne that noman knoweth but thei, and therfore mowe thei not gon out. And also thee schull understonde that the Iewes han no propre lond of hire owne for to dwellen inne in all the world, but only that lond betwene the mountaynes.[40]

The *Travels* also insists here that the Jews have persisted in this seemingly counterproductive monolingualism in order to be able to recognize each other as fellow conspirators in the last days:

> And thit natheless men seyn thei schull gon out in the tyme of Antecrist and that thei schull maken gret slaughter of cristene men, and therfore all the Iewes that dwellen in all londes lernen all weys to speken Ebrew, in hope that whan the other Iewes schull gone out, that thei may understonden hire speche and to leden hem in to cristendom for to destroye the cristene peple. For the Iewes seyn that thei knowen wel be hire prophecyes that thei of Caspye schull gon out and spreden throgh out all the world. And that the cristene men schull ben under hire subieccioun als longe as thei han ben in subieccioun of hem.[41]

The spoken Hebrew (could the narrator of the *Travels* be recognizing emergent Yiddish?) in the "East" of the *Travels* thus begins to collide with the Hebrew alphabet located by the narrator in the "West." One suspects that the author saw a gap between "classical" or scriptural languages and the spoken language of medieval Jews in northern Europe. Whereas the *Travels* uses alphabets to guarantee "Western" civilization and the stars to explain "natural" (Eastern) diversity, this division of labor in the text breaks down with spoken Hebrew, which the narrator maps in the space of the apocalypse (Gog and Magog) and casts as a language of conspiracy, a technology of Antichrist. Hebrew is thus modelled as a language of a people doomed to be a "who you are," a people excluded from the *Travels'* tolerant diversity of "where you are." Jews interrupt the so-called "rational" tolerance of the text. If, according to Greenblatt, the narrator "takes possession of nothing,"[42] it does not mean that he refrains from dispossession. Secure in his rationalism, in the "lettres"[43] that guarantee him access to forbidden places, the narrator of the *Travels* can continue the medieval Christian rational project of dispossessing the Jews, this time layering the astrolabe with spoken Hebrew.

The *Travels* is certainly not the first medieval text to play with alphabets; significantly for my argument, however, it produces its practices of inclusion and exclusion through their staging. It uncouples the alphabet from its acoustical/graphic modalities in order to map letters as territory itself. The letters thus become cartographic codes.[44] The

Travels uses the alphabet to represent the space of territory, not the time of reading and writing. Such cartographic use of alphabets actually comes from the astrolabe, which serves as the model for such coding.

Let me pause here to show how the alphabet becomes part of an astronomical machine. At the time of composing the *Travels* astrolabes were commonly used to tell time as Figure 4, a reproduction of a diagram from Geoffrey Chaucer's essay on the astrolabe, illustrates. Readers of the *Travels* who wished to tell time with the astrolabe would find themselves using the alphabet as a code. Telling time with this instrument involved the cross-correlation of the altitude of the sun read from the rule on the backside of the astrolabe with the positioning of the rete to correspond to the date of the reading on its frontside. The pointer on the label would then fall on one of 23 capital letters of the alphabet, or a cross, which marked 15-degree increments of the 24-hour day on the outer border of the astrolabe. The user would then count off the positions of the letters to arrive at the hour of the day.[45] The alphabet thus came to share in the mechanicity of the astrolabe. It was inscribed as a code on a portable object with moveable parts. The reading of the code is a repeatable procedure; and the alphabet encodes time as spatial demarcation. The *Travels* mobilizes the alphabet code of the astrolabe to mechanize human diversity.

So far I have suggested that the strategic invocation of scientific rationalism in the form of astronomical discourse on longitude and latitude, grounded in the use of the astrolabe, emerges at critical moments of encounter with Jews in the work of Petrus Alfonsi and *Mandeville's Travels*. The *Travels* not only uses that strand of rationalism but also incorporates the apocalyptic cartography of the Victorines, who in spite of their purported tolerance linked Jews with the peoples of Gog and Magog and the fantasized annihilation of Christians at the hands of the Jews in the last days. The *Travels* goes even further. Not only does the narrator of Mandeville measure with the astrolabe, he also transfers its alphabetical code as he textualizes territory. Like the alphabetical code on the astrolabe, alphabets in the *Travels* are cartographical codes that excise the alphabet from the particular temporalities of reading words. Human diversity in the *Travels* thus becomes a kind of mechanized universalism. Only a secret, spoken language, Hebrew, escapes this coding at the cost of intolerance.[46]

These different "rational" moments attest to the violence that can lurk in between time and space in medieval mapping practices. I now wish to consider, at last, the printed editions of Ptolemy's *Geography*, along with Christian-Hebrew studies that developed just as the *Geography* came to press. What might seem separate endeavors, cartography and humanist philology, I argue are intimately intertwined in

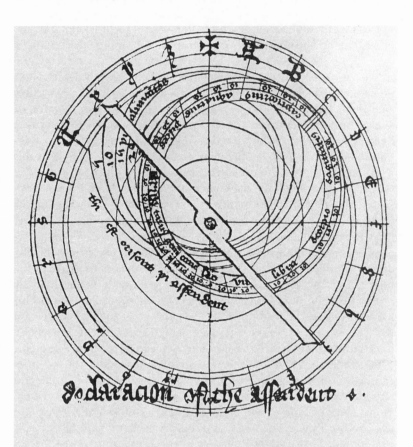

3. To knowe euery tyme of the day by liht of the sonne, and euery
tyme of the nyht by the sterres fixe, and eke to knowe by nyht
or by day the degree of any signe that assendith on the est
Orisonte, which that is cleped communly the assendent or elles
oruscupum.

[*Ad cognoscendum quidlibet tempus diei per solis indicacionem, et
quodlibet tempus noctis per quasdam stellas in celo fixas; ac eciam
ad inveniendum et cognoscendum signum super orizontem qui
communiter vocatur ascendens.*]

Figure 4. Illustration from Chaucer's lesson on telling time with the astrolabe.
MS Cambridge Dd.3.53. By permission of the Syndics of Cambridge University Library.

intensifying detemporalization of contemporary Jews. Put another way, it is not surprising to see Christian intellectuals, such as Pico della Mirandola, deeply involved in Jewish Kabbala *and* Ptolemaic geography. What Michael Taussig has described for a New World colonial context as the "search for the White Indian," I appropriate here as the "search for the classic Jew" or the "Jew of Hebrew Scripture" (that is, the pre-crucifixion Jew, not the Talmud Jew of medieval Northern Europe). By the latter part of the fifteenth century the Christian typological imaginary repetitiously incarnated the "Talmud Jew" (whom they had so radically detemporalized) into mechanical reproduction, that is, into printing itself.[47]

The ABC of Ptolemy: The Alphabet as Territory

Changes in script and the reception of the *Geography* in the fifteenth century are closely bound. Humanists gridded the letters of the alphabet just as they gridded cartographic space. The difference a grid makes can be exemplified by comparing two alphabets, one dating from 1460, the alphabet of Marie de Bourgogne, and the other from 1480, known as the alphabet of Damianus Moyllus.[48] This alphabet is the first printed version of an alphabet in Roman font. A manuscript treatise on the design of the Roman alphabet, written by Felice Feliciano (1460–63) at the same time as the execution of the Gothic alphabet of Marie de Bourgogne, did not make its way into print. The differences between the Gothic and Roman alphabets are starkly drawn. Compare the letter "M" of the de Bourgogne alphabet (Figure 5) with the letter "A" of the Moyllus alphabet (Figure 6). The "M" seems to pun acoustically on "M" for "mâchoire" or jaw. The jaw is drawn in the resemblance of the clitoris, the orifices burst out of the elaborated, fragmented frame of the gothic letter, as if genitals gird the dissolving ductus of this letter. The Roman letters of the Moyllus alphabet, in contrast, are "constructed" from the principles of geometry. The letter "A" features none of the acoustical punning or anthropomorphizing typical of the de Bourgogne letters. The letters of the Roman alphabet materialize within their own self-sufficient geometric grid. So constructed, Roman type effaced its own historicity to produce a timeless, monumental space, cleansed of the corporeal excess of the de Bourgogne letter.

Historians of the Roman font trace the design to the courts of the Este in Ferrara and the Gonzaga in Mantua. It is also at the Este court where astrologers approved Nicolaus Germanus's manuscript edition of Ptolemy, which served as the exemplar for the printed Ulm editions of 1482 and 1486. Printers of an incunabular *Geography* consistently set the text in the Roman alphabet. Their choice of typeface, I want to argue, is more than just a "style." Rather, the choice to print with Roman typeface complemented the refiguring of temporality encoded in the gridded cartographic space of the maps that travelled with the *Geography*. Let me turn to a detailed discussion of a printed edition of the *Geography* to expand on this claim.

"Rediscovered" in its translation from Greek into Latin in 1405–1409, Ptolemy's *Geography* presented its students with a practical guide to constructing maps on a grid of longitude and latitude and offered a list of these coordinates for over 8,000 place-names, grouped by the imperial regions current in the late antique world.[49] A work much

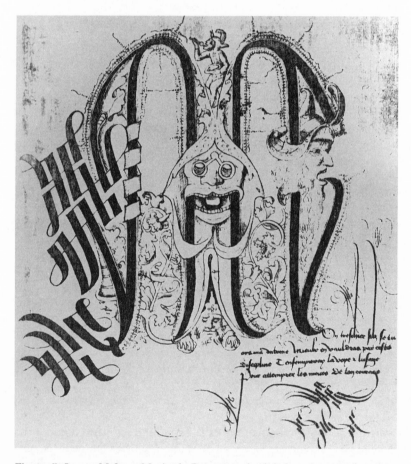

Figure 5. Letter M from Marie de Bourgogne's alphabet. As reproduced in Pierre Dumon, *L'Alphabet gothique dit de Marie de Bourgogne: Reproduction du codex Bruxellensis II 845* (Antwerp: De Nederlandsche Boekhandel, 1973).

Queſto :A:ſi caua del tondo & del quadro:Lagá
ba da man dricta uole eſſere de le :xii:parte una
de lalteza del quadro:Lagamba da man ſiniſtra
piu ſubtile:la mitade de la groſſa gamba:Et que
la dimezi piu ſubtile:Et debe eſſere uno terzo de
la ganba grofa:Lalteza de queſto:A :& ſua large
za ſi pigliano inſu la croce del tondo in trinſeca
to da le linie che deriuano da li anguli del qua´
dro :Et lultima linia de lagamba pin ſubtile uo
le eſſere una goſeza de la gamba groſſa ſoto el cé
tro como qui apare :& : c :

Figure 6. Letter A from the Damianus Moyllus alphabet, Parma. As reproduced in Stanley Morison, ed., *The Moyllus Alphabet: A Newly Discovered Treatise
on Classic Letter Design Printed at Parma c. 1480* (New York: Pegasus, 1927).

published by Italian and German printers, an edition of a *Geography* staked a cultural claim for the publisher's city in trans-European print culture. Each edition of the *Geography* became what Lisa Jardine has termed "the basis for further collaborative attention, repersonalising and revivifying the 'dead letter' of the printed page."[50] The front and back matter, especially indices, began to accrete around these different printed iterations of the *Geography*. Such editorial elaborations changed the ways readers might read the text. Francesco Berlinghieri's vernacular verse adaptation of Ptolemy, for example, was the first edition (Florence 1482) to include *tabulae novellae*, or updated maps, in this instance for Spain, France, Italy, and the Holy Land. Berlinghieri's edition also included new front matter that aided the reader's navigation through the Ptolemaic treatise. On folio 2r of this edition the Ptolemaic regions were alphabetized (from Achaia to Vindelicia), after which the relevant book, chapter, and map number were listed for each regional name. This edition also alphabetized the place-names of each region at the end of each book and then listed the respective longitude and latitude. The maps for each region were placed after each book. This editorial apparatus thus used the different chapter or "book" divisions as its basic organizational unit and alphabetized information with reference to each of its books.[51]

The 1486 edition of the *Geography* printed at Ulm (the second edition to be printed north of the Alps) shows the treatise on the way to becoming an atlas, a cartographic genre that would achieve its full commercial success in the sixteenth century. This edition is notable for several reasons. First, like all previous editions including its prototype, the 1482 Ulm edition, it is printed in Roman type, the typeface of choice for "scientific" texts.[52] (The mathematician Regiomontanus and Hermann Schedel of Nuremberg had just introduced the typeface to German presses north of the Alps.[53]) The printer of the 1486 Ptolemy recycled the woodcut maps of the 1482 edition, but made significant additions to the front and back matter of the volume. Most importantly, elaborating on and significantly rearranging the editorial aids of Berlinghieri, the 1486 Ulm Ptolemy included an alphabetized register of places, *Registrum alphabeticum super octo libros Ptolomaei* as prefatory material to the *Geography*. This *Registrum* was compiled from each of the indices of the regional books (Books 2–7) and was accompanied by cross-listings of the number of the map on which the place could be located. A brief descriptive annotation accompanied many of the alphabetized places.[54] Thenceforth, editions of the *Geography* would travel with front and back matter.[55] This seemingly mundane *Registrum alphabeticum* had powerful, if unintended, effects as an editorial apparatus. By alphabetizing all places without regard to the book-by-book regional divisions, this edition stripped the *Geography* of time, the timing of reading and browsing through the treatise. It superimposed instead an alphabetical list, or grid, onto a cartographic grid of longitude and latitude.[56] Readers could locate the name of a place in the alphabetic list at the front of the volume and then could simply turn to the relevant map at the back of the volume to verify its cartographic location. The alphabetical list of places and map references meant that it was no longer necessary, as it had been prior to their introduction, to peruse the chapters of the *Geography* in order to link a place with a map. By the time of publication of the Strassburg edition of 1513, this editorial tool had reached its empirical minimalism in the form of a long list of alphabetized places (culled from the Ptolemaic maps) and cross-listed with their longitude and latitude (Figure 7). The effect of this apparatus was to make the *Geography* work like an atlas before the production of atlases (a phenomenon of the mid-sixteenth century).

In addition, the 1486 Ptolemy is also the first edition to append a short treatise after the maps entitled "on three parts of the world and the various men, portents and transformations with rivers, islands and mountains." Using excerpts from the work of Isidore and Vincent of Beauvais, it offered readers familiar encyclopedic fare typically associated with *mappaemundi*.[57] In sum, the 1486 Ptolemy layers a range of complex material: Roman typeface as signifier of the "scientific" content of the *Geography*, an alphabetized register of places cross-referenced to their respective maps (a tool that enables the book to work more like an atlas), and finally, a seemingly atavistic encyclopedic tract on the wonders of the world.

The *Registrum*, so conceived, marked the use of alphabetization as an increasingly effective indexing tool for cartography. The alphabet grid indexed to longitude and latitude produced a matrix with ramifications for processes of detemporalization under discussion in this essay.[58] It might be argued that since Ptolemaic maps did not grid apocalyptic space, that they would seem to arrest processes of detemporalization. Indeed, by "cleansing" cartographical space of the apocalypse and by cleansing the alphabet of the overdetermined territorial coding noted in the *Travels*, Ptolemaic maps might be understood as agents of amnesia that erased evidence of a troubling history of detemporalizing Jews—the entangled layers so far discussed of Gog and Magog, the Hebrew alphabet, and the Hebrew language. In pondering this, it is important to remember that Ptolemaic maps did not circulate in isolation from other humanist projects. These maps need to be considered in terms of new arguments about philology made in Christian-Hebrew studies.

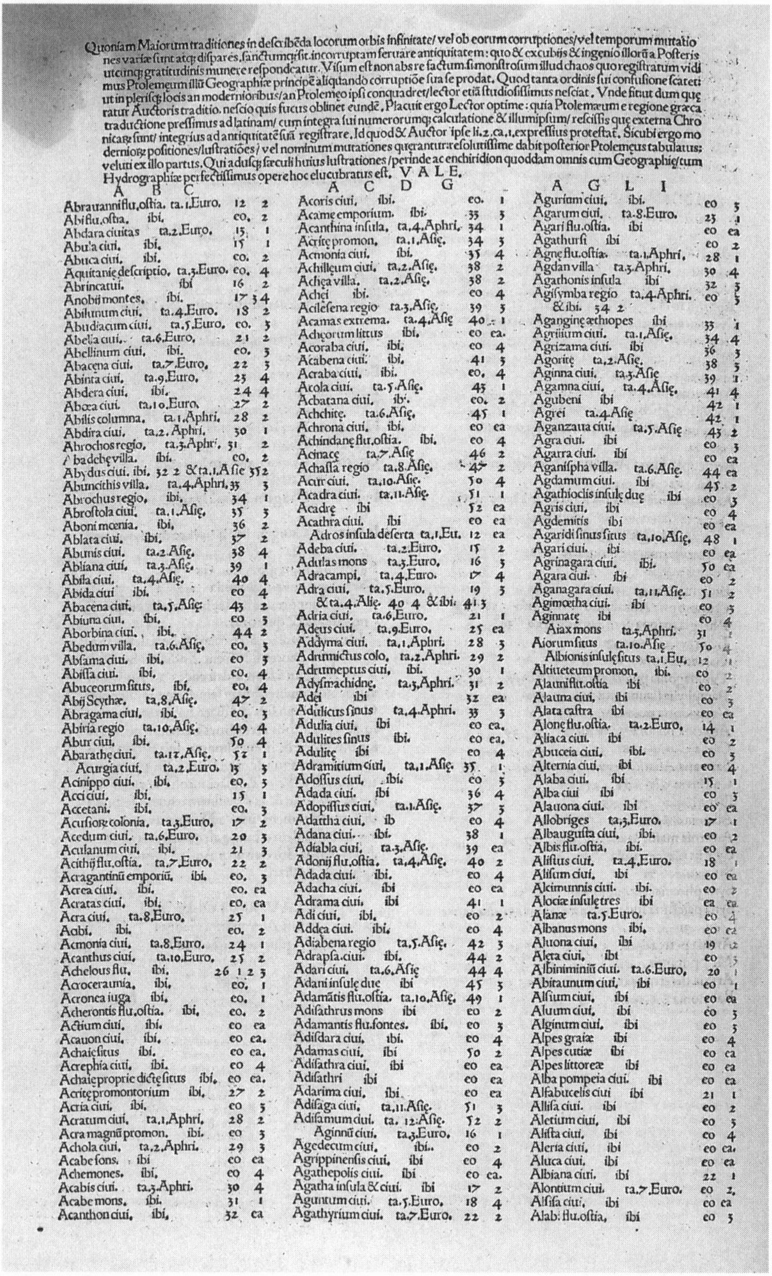

Quoniam Maiorum traditiones in deſcribēda locorum orbis infinitate/ vel ob eorum corruptiones/vel temporum mutatio nes variæ ſunt atq; diſpares, ſanctumq; ſit incorruptam ſeruare antiquitatem: quo & excubijs & ingenio illorū a Poſteris utcunq; gratitudinis munere reſpondeatur. Viſum eſt non abs re ſactum ſi monſtroſum illud chaos quo regiſtratum vidi mus Ptolemęum illū Geographiæ principē aliquando corruptiōe ſua ſe prodat. Quod tanta ordinis ſui confuſione ſcateti ut in pleriſq; locis an modernioribus/an Ptolemęo ipſi conquadret/lector etiā ſtudioſiſſimus neſciat. Vnde ſitut dum quę ratur Auctoris traditio. neſcio quis fucus oblinet eundē. Placuit ergo Lector optime: quia Ptolemæum e regione græca traductione preſſimus ad latinam/ cum integra ſui numerorumq; calculatione & illumipſum/ reſciſſis quę externa Chro nicarū ſunt/ integrius ad antiquitatē ſuā regiſtrare. Id quod & Auctor ipſe li.2.ca.1.expreſſius proteſtat. Sicubi ergo mo derniorū poſitiones/luſtratiōes/ vel nominum mutationes quęrantur: reſolutiſſime dabit poſterior Ptolemęus tabulatus: veluti ex illo partus. Qui aduſq; ſæculi huius luſtrationes /perinde ac enchiridion quoddam omnis cum Geographię/tum Hydrographiæ perfectiſſimus opere hoc elucubratus eſt. V A L E.

A B C

Abrauanniflu.oſtia.	ta.1.Euro.	12	2
Abiflu.oſtra.	ibi.	eo.	2
Abdara ciuitas	ta.2.Euro.	15	1
Abu'a ciui.	ibi.	15	1
Abuca ciui.	ibi.	eo.	2
Aquitanię deſcriptio.	ta.3.Euro.	eo.	4
Abrincatui.	ibi	16	2
Anobij montes.	ibi.	17	34
Abilunum ciui.	ta.4.Euro.	18	2
Abudiacum ciui.	ta.5.Euro.	eo.	3
Abella ciui.	ta.6.Euro.	21	2
Abellinum ciui.	ibi.	eo.	3
Abacena ciui.	ta.7.Euro.	22	3
Abinta ciui.	ta.9.Euro.	23	4
Abdera ciui.	ibi.	24	4
Abœa ciui.	ta.10.Euro.	27	2
Abilis columna.	ta.1.Aphri.	28	2
Abdira ciui.	ta.2.Aphri.	30	1
Abrochos regio.	ta.3.Aphri.	31	2
Abadchę villa.	ibi.	eo.	2
Abydus ciui. ibi. 32 2 & ta.1.Aſie		35	2
Abuncithis villa.	ta.4.Aphri.	33	3
Abrochus regio.	ibi.	34	1
Abroſtola ciui.	ta.1.Aſię.	35	3
Aboni mœnia.	ibi.	36	2
Ablata ciui.	ibi.	37	2
Abunis ciui.	ta.2.Aſię.	38	4
Abliana ciui.	ta.3.Aſię.	39	1
Abila ciui.	ta.4.Aſię.	40	4
Abida ciui	ibi.	eo	4
Abacena ciui.	ta.5.Aſię.	43	2
Abiuna ciui.	ibi.	eo	3
Aborbina ciui.	ibi.	44	2
Abedum villa.	ta.6.Aſię.	eo.	3
Abſama ciui.	ibi.	eo	3
Abiſſa ciui.	ibi.	eo.	4
Abuceorum ſitus.	ibi.	eo.	4
Abij Scythæ.	ta.8.Aſię.	47	2
Abragama ciui.	ibi.	eo.	3
Abiria regio	ta.10.Aſię.	49	4
Abur ciui.	ibi.	50	4
Abarathę ciui.	ta.12.Aſię.	52	1
Acurgia ciui.	ta.2.Euro.	15	3
Acinippo ciui.	ibi.	eo.	3
Acci ciui.	ibi.	15	1
Accetani.	ibi.	eo.	3
Acuſiorū colonia.	ta.3.Euro.	17	2
Acedum ciui.	ta.6.Euro.	20	3
Aculanum ciui.	ibi.	21	3
Acithij flu.oſtia.	ta.7.Euro.	22	2
Acragantinū emporiū.	ibi.	eo.	3
Acrea ciui.	ibi.	eo.	ea
Acratas ciui.	ibi.	eo.	ea
Acra ciui.	ta.8.Euro.	25	1
Acabi.	ibi.	eo.	2
Acmonia ciui.	ta.8.Euro.	24	1
Acanthus ciui.	ta.10.Euro.	25	2
Achelous flu.	ibi.	26	1 2 3
Acroceraunia.	ibi.	eo.	1
Acronca iuga	ibi.	eo.	1
Acherontis flu.oſtia.	ibi.	eo.	2
Actium ciui.	ibi.	eo	ea
Acauon ciui.	ibi.	eo	ea.
Achaieſitus	ibi.	eo	ea.
Acrephia ciui.	ibi.	eo	4
Achaię proprie dictę ſitus	ibi.	eo	ea.
Acritę promontorium	ibi.	27	2
Acria ciui.	ibi.	eo	3
Acratum ciui.	ta.1.Aphri.	28	2
Acra magnū promon.	ibi.	eo	3
Achola ciui.	ta.2.Aphri.	29	3
Acabe ſons.	ibi	eo	ea
Achemones.	ibi.	eo	4
Acabis ciui.	ta.3.Aphri.	30	4
Acabe mons.	ibi.	31	1
Acanthon ciui.	ibi.	32	ea

A C D G

Acoris ciui.	ibi.	eo.	1
Acamę emporium.	ibi.	33	3
Acanthina inſula.	ta.4.Aphri.	34	1
Acritę promon.	ta.1.Aſię.	34	3
Acmonia ciui.	ibi.	35	4
Achillęum ciui.	ta.2.Aſię.	38	2
Achęa villa.	ta.2.Aſię.	38	2
Achęi	ibi.	eo	4
Acileſena regio	ta.3.Aſię.	39	3
Acamas extrema.	ta.4.Aſię	40	1
Achęorum littus	ibi.	eo	ea.
Acoraba ciui.	ibi.	eo	4
Acabena ciui.	ibi.	41	3
Acraba ciui.	ibi.	eo.	4
Acola ciui.	ta.5.Aſię.	43	1
Acbatana ciui.	ibi.	eo.	2
Achchitę.	ta.6.Aſię.	45	1
Achrona ciui.	ibi.	eo	ea
Achindanę flu.oſtia.	ibi.	eo	4
Acinacę	ta.7.Aſię	46	2
Achaſſa regio	ta.8.Aſię.	47	2
Acur ciui.	ta.10.Aſię.	50	4
Acadra ciui.	ta.11.Aſię.	51	1
Acadrę	ibi	52	ea
Acathra ciui.	ibi	eo	ea
Adros inſula deſerta	ta.1.Eu.	12	ea
Adeba ciui.	ta.2.Euro.	15	2
Adulas mons	ta.3.Euro.	16	3
Adracampi.	ta.4.Euro.	17	4
Adra ciui.	ta.5.Euro.	19	3
& ta.4.Aſię. 40 4 & ibi.		41	3
Adria ciui.	ta.6.Euro.	21	1
Adęus ciui.	ta.9.Euro.	25	ea
Addyma ciui.	ta.1.Aphri.	28	3
Adrumictus colo.	ta.2.Aphri.	29	2
Adrumeptus ciui.	ibi.	30	1
Adyſmachidnę.	ta.3.Aphri.	31	2
Adęi	ibi	32	ea
Adulicus ſinus	ta.4.Aphri.	33	3
Adulia ciui.	ibi	eo	ea.
Adulites ſinus	ibi.	eo	ea.
Adulitę	ibi	eo	4
Adramitium ciui.	ta.1.Aſię.	35	1
Adoſſus ciui.	ibi.	eo	3
Adada ciui.	ibi	36	4
Adopiſſus ciui.	ta.1.Aſię.	37	3
Adattha ciui.	ib	eo	4
Adana ciui.	ibi.	38	1
Adiabla ciui.	ta.3.Aſię.	39	ea
Adonij flu.oſtia.	ta.4.Aſię.	40	2
Adada ciui.	ibi.	eo	4
Adacha ciui.	ibi	eo	ea
Adrama ciui.	ibi	41	1
Adi ciui.	ibi.	eo	2
Addęa ciui.	ibi.	eo	4
Adiabena regio	ta.5.Aſię.	42	3
Adrapſa ciui.	ibi.	44	2
Adari ciui.	ta.6.Aſię	44	4
Adani inſulę due	ibi	45	3
Adamātis flu.oſtia.	ta.10.Aſię.	49	1
Adiſathrus mons	ibi	eo	2
Adamantis flu.fontes.	ibi.	eo	3
Adiſdara ciui.	ibi.	eo	4
Adamas ciui.	ibi	50	2
Adiſathra ciui.	ibi	eo	ea
Adiſathri	ibi	eo	ea
Adarima ciui.	ibi	eo	ea
Adiſaga ciui.	ta.11.Aſię.	51	3
Adiſamum ciui.	ta.12.Aſię.	52	2
Aginnū ciui.	ta.3.Euro.	16	1
Agedecum ciui.	ibi..	eo	2
Agrippinenſis ciui.	ibi	eo	4
Agathepolis ciui.	ibi	eo	ea.
Agatha inſula & ciui.	ibi	17	2
Aguntum ciui.	ta.5.Euro.	18	4
Agathyrium ciui.	ta.7.Euro.	22	2

A G L I

Agurium ciui.	ibi.	eo	3
Agarum ciui.	ta.8.Euro.	23	1
Agari flu.oſtia.	ibi	eo	ea
Agathurſi	ibi	eo	2
Agnę flu.oſtia.	ta.1.Aphri.	28	1
Agdan villa	ta.3.Aphri.	30	4
Agathonis inſula	ibi	32	3
Agiſymba regio	ta.4.Aphri.	eo	3
& ibi. 54 2			
Agangine æthiopes	ibi	33	1
Agriium ciui.	ta.1.Aſię.	34	4
Agrizama ciui.	ibi	36	3
Agoritę	ta.2.Aſię.	38	3
Aginna ciui.	ta.3.Aſię	39	1
Agamna ciui.	ta.4.Aſię.	41	4
Agubeni	ibi	42	1
Agrei	ta.4.Aſię	42	1
Aganzaua ciui.	ta.5.Aſię	43	2
Agra ciui.	ibi	eo	3
Agarra ciui.	ibi	eo	ea
Aganiſpha villa.	ta.6.Aſię.	44	ea
Agdamum ciui.	ibi	45	2
Agathioclis inſulę duę	ibi	eo	3
Agris ciui.	ibi	eo	4
Agdemitis	ibi	eo	ea
Agaridi ſinus ſitus	ta.10.Aſię.	48	1
Agari ciui.	ibi	eo	ea
Agrinagara ciui.	ibi.	50	ea
Agara ciui.	ibi	eo	2
Aganagara ciui.	ta.11.Aſię.	51	2
Agimœtha ciui.	ibi	eo	3
Aginnatę	ibi	eo	4
Aiax mons	ta.3.Aphri.	31	1
Aiorum ſitus	ta.10.Aſię	50	4
Albionis inſulę ſitus	ta.1.Eu.	12	1
Altiueteum promon.	ibi.	eo	2
Alauni flu.oſtia	ibi	eo	2
Alauna ciui.	ibi	eo	3
Alata caſtra	ibi	eo	ea
Alonę flu.oſtia.	ta.2.Euro.	14	1
Aliaca ciui.	ibi	eo	2
Abuceia ciui.	ibi.	eo	3
Alternia ciui.	ibi	eo	4
Alaba ciui.	ibi	15	1
Alba ciui	ibi	eo	3
Alauona ciui.	ibi	eo	ea
Allobriges	ta.3.Euro.	17	1
Albaugusta ciui.	ibi.	eo	2
Albis flu.oſtia.	ibi.	eo	ea
Aliſtus ciui.	ta.4.Euro.	18	1
Aliſum ciui.	ibi	eo	ea
Alcimunnis ciui.	ibi.	eo	2
Alociæ inſulę tres	ibi	ea	ea
Alanæ	ta.5.Euro.	eo	4
Albanus mons	ibi.	eo	ea
Aluona ciui.	ibi	19	2
Alęta ciui.	ibi	eo	3
Albiniminiū ciui.	ta.6.Euro.	20	1
Abitaunum ciui.	ibi	eo	1
Alſium ciui.	ibi	eo	ea
Aluum ciui.	ibi	eo	3
Alginum ciui.	ibi	eo	3
Alpes graiæ	ibi	eo	4
Alpes cutiæ	ibi	eo	ea
Alpes littoreæ	ibi	eo	ea
Alba pompeia ciui.	ibi	eo	ea
Alfabucelis ciui	ibi	21	1
Alliſa ciui.	ibi	eo	2
Aletium ciui.	ibi	eo	3
Aliſta ciui.	ibi	eo	4
Aleria ciui.	ibi	eo	ea.
Aluca ciui.	ibi	eo	ea
Albiana ciui.	ibi	22	1
Alontium ciui.	ta.7.Euro.	eo	2.
Alſiſa ciui.	ibi	eo	ea
Alab: flu.oſtia.	ibi	eo	3

Figure 7. First page of alphabetical register of places and coordinates from Ptolemy, *Geographie opus nouissima traductione* (Argentina). Courtesy of the Rare Books Division, New York Public Library, Astor, Lennox, and Tilden Foundations.

Classical Christianity and the "Classic" Jew

The project of alphabetizing space and using the alphabet as a tool to map places coincided significantly within another humanist project, that of Christian-Hebrew studies. The mid-fifteenth century saw a renewed interest in the philological study of Hebrew scriptures and Kaballa among humanist scholars. These humanists were especially interested in the classicizing notion of a "prisca theologia." They wished to recuperate an original Jewish antiquity prior to Jewish refusal of Christ as messiah. They also saw their work as a philological salvage mission designed to rescue the Hebrew scriptures from what they claimed to be the ignorance of contemporary Jews who, they argued, did not have the appropriate skills to deal with their own sacred text. So argued the Florentine Hebraist Giannozzo Manetti (1396–1459) in response to serious accusations of judaizing. The work of Christian-Hebrew studies would, according to Manetti, save the Psalter from the obstinacy of the Jews.[59] Manetti's defense marked one strand of Christian-Hebrew studies as imperial and appropriating rather than cooperative and tolerant—let humanist Christians undertake what contemporary rabbis were too philologically benighted to do properly. Thus Christian-Hebrew studies as a rationalized humanistic undertaking honed a sharp edge against the Jews, using Hebrew as a weapon against them.

Translation of the Old Testament from Hebrew to Latin was not the only strand of Christian-Hebrew studies. The encounter of humanist philologists with Jewish mysticism was also compelling. Just as the Ulm 1486 edition of Ptolemy appeared, Pico della Mirandola finished his 900 conclusions on the Kabbala. In a theological family tree Kabbala provided for Pico the "missing link" between "prisca theologica," that is, pre-crucifixion Judaism, and Christian revelation.[60] Pico thus sought to map a new "missing link" for Christendom, that of a "real" classic Jewish body, infused with wisdom and untainted by the obstinacy of refusing to recognize Christ.[61] Pico constructs this phantasmatic body just as coeval medieval Talmud Jews were expelled at last from medieval mapping practices, and, increasingly, from medieval territories as well. What is the significance of this "classic" Jewish body, a missing Jewish link, imagined and possessed by Christian-Hebrew studies in the latter half of the fifteenth century—a body that is invented as editions of Ptolemy's *Geography* roll off the press?

The ritual murder trial held in the city of Trent in 1475 can exemplify the crucial stakes at issue in this question. In that year, town magistrates arrested all eighteen resident Jewish men and one Jewish woman to investigate the purported ritual murder of a two-year-old

Christian boy, Simon. The inquest and torture of these men and woman and the executions of the male Jews occurred at the crossroads of Italy and Germany, of humanist and scholastic thought, of local and papal contests, coincidentally at the very time that editions of Ptolemy's *Geography* were coming to press. Supporters of the trial and the cult of the boy-martyr Simon used the press (Latin and vernacular) to disseminate their propaganda. The extracted narrative of the trial record and the popular, printed iconography of Simon dwell on his circumcision at the hands of these Jews (Figure 8).[62] The executed bodies of these Trent Jews, who died as persecution of Jews intensified in northern Italy and southern Germany in the latter part of the fifteenth century, need to be joined with the missing Jewish link, the "classic" Jew, imagined by philologists such as Pico.

The Trent corpses and the fantasy of the "classic" Jew come together over rituals of verification. Medieval Christians had relied on the body of the Jew to authorize the integrity of their chief ritual, the Eucharist. The Christians believed that the Jews' handling of the host could make it bleed, testimony of its cultic holiness. Moreover, only Jews could ritually circumcise a Christian boy to produce a facsimile of

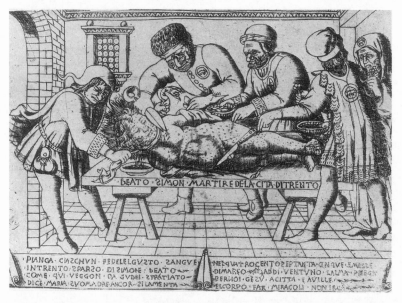

Figure 8. Artist unknown (probably Florentine), *The Ritual Murder of S. Simon of Trent*, ca. 1475–85. Reproduced from Arthur M. Hind, ed., *Florentine Engravings and Anonymous Prints of Other Schools*, part 1 of *Early Italian Engraving*, vol. 2 (1938; reprint New York: Kraus, 1970), pl. 74. Photograph courtesy of the Getty Center.

a little Christ for cultic (and lucrative) Christian relic worship.[63] Christian-Hebraists were using scholarly practices and new printing technologies to change these rituals of verification. Rather than have living "Talmud" Jews guarantee the efficacy of the Eucharist as a sacrament, instead these philologists, in an act of excessive philological mimesis that guaranteed their philology as a new textual sacrament, circumcised the Hebrew alphabet. In graphically reterritorializing the study of the Hebrew alphabet as a mathematical and philological science, philologists drained it of its blood, so to speak, just at the moment that their counterparts prosecuted Jews in inquisitorial courts for draining young, male Christians—and Christendom itself —of blood. Printing helped to disseminate rituals of verification.

Printing helped constitute but did not technologically determine the further detemporalization of European Jews. As humanistic studies shifted their anxious need for origins to print-related activities, they concomitantly diminished their need for sacramental presence to authorize symbols. Thus, the dissemination of a *printed* Christendom further enabled the expulsion and persecution of contempory Jews, since the antique "classic" Jew, as a graphic phenomenon, could be much more reliably constructed, reproduced, and disseminated through print. Jews were becoming graphically reduced to "paper Jews" for Christians. Hence the corporeal expulsion of Jews from humanist spaces has much to do with the mechanical reproduction and, more importantly, with the dissemination of print media during the first print-century. These emerging media provided the opportunity to construct a seemingly timeless antique Jewish origin that could be controlled, circulated, and reproduced. Thus guaranteed of an origin, cartographic space could become seemingly timeless, as it did in the Ulm 1486 edition of Ptolemy's *Geography*.

Such a totalizing gesture, is, however, never truly verifiable. Perhaps that is why the 1486 edition, anxiously, appends to itself the small tract on marvels and wonders. Perhaps, too, this is why the world map by John Ruysch, which was published among the *tabulae novae* of the Rome Ptolemy of 1508, located "iudei inclusi" in northern Greenland. The apocalyptic Jews return for a moment on the Ruysch map, which Nordenskiöld describes as "not a copy of the map of the world by Ptolemy, nor a learned master-piece composed at the writing-table, but a revision of the old maps of the known world, made on a Ptolemaic, i.e., on a scientific basis."[64]

Just as Petrus Alfonsi would colonize the place of the geographic observer by excluding Jews from it; just as Mandeville declared their language "not quite, not right" among "Western" alphabets, thus excluding Jews from the scriptural territory of civilization; so did a strand of humanist philology expel Jews from the expertise of Christian-Hebraic studies. Their Hebrew language could be turned against them through a philological technology. Ptolemy's widely disseminated *Geography*, published in Northern Europe with its apparatus of alphabetized places in Roman font, "cleansed" the space of the medieval world map and produced through the alphabet a territory which would refigure space, old and new, for colonization. Thus it can be said that the modernist fiction of the stand-alone map stands on displaced and dead bodies, real (such as the dead Jews of the Trent ritual murder trial) and phantasmatic (the "Talmud" Jew). The chastening of space in the Ptolemaic project did the graphic work that paved the way for the intensification of Jewish expulsions in the late fifteenth century.

This double-barreled technology, alphabet as territory, cartography as alphabet, helped to spread the carnage so notable in that mid-millennium. Upon its export to the New World this cartographic technology produced, yet again, catastrophic effects, as the work of Walter Mignolo and others in *Writing Without Words* has taught us.[65] The power of alphabetical cartography persists even today, albeit very much embedded, in the Human Genome Project, a scriptural mapping technology par excellence.[66] An understanding of cartographic genealogies and their typological hauntings, as I have tried to outline here, can contribute to the urgent political task of refiguring power in contemporary cartographies, even at the molecular level.

Chapter 2
Printing Excision:
The Graphic Afterlife of
Medieval Universal Histories

A Secret Room

On December 29, 1491, a wealthy Nuremberg merchant, Sebald
Schreyer, and his brother-in-law, Sebastian Kammermeister, signed
a contract with the "painters" Michael Wolgemut and Wilhelm Pley-
denwurff for the production of the *Nuremberg Chronicle*, a printed universal history conceived to out-compete in sheer size and number of
illustrations (1,809 illustrations printed from 654 blocks) a number
of other popular printed histories already on the European market.
Secrecy was to shroud the printing process. Another contract, signed
in March 1492 with the Nuremberg printer Anton Koberger, whose
printing house was then one of the largest in Europe, required him to
"reserve and make available . . . a special room in [his] house, in
which . . . [they] are able to put together, arrange, and keep the block
for the illustrations . . . to see that nothing of these books and illustrations will be printed, proofed, or taken away in the knowledge and
wish of the above-mentioned persons."[1] Such a secret room is intriguing. Within it, printers used moveable type and woodcuts to break
up the familiar traditional time lines that had been devised to bind
together the narrative of medieval universal history. By setting the
familiar and traditional genre of universal history into a new graphic
format, the printers of the *Nuremberg Chronicle* remapped the hermeneutic divide of supersession. Where initially the typological imaginary
had located supersession *between* the Hebrew Bible and the New Testament, now a new graphics emergent in the late fifteenth century represented the divide *within* the Old Testament itself. Incunabular print
culture graphed a new hermeneutical divide and thus transformed

the reader of such images before Luther preached it.[2] At stake was a reconfigured supersession in which Christians became the members of the faithful synagogue (fidelis synagoga). And crucial to the understanding of such a typological dynamic is the process whereby the faithful synagogue phantasmatically reoccupied the mystical body (corpus mysticum) of the Catholic Church. Where the corpus mysticum had been, there was now the fidelis synagoga. This chapter traces the graphic work that materialized Christian reoccupation of the synagogue and its implication for Jews in the typological imaginary.

Universal Histories as Genre

Most scholars regard the *Nuremberg Chronicle*, which came off the press on July 12, 1493, as a quintessentially medieval artifact. They imagine the *Chronicle* rather in the way scholars have thought about medieval *mappaemundi* in relation to the maps of Ptolemy's *Geography*. In Chapter 1 I explored the problems with such supersessionary thinking in cartography. This chapter finds similar problems with any quick dismissal of the *Nuremberg Chronicle* as familiarly medieval. As a universal history, it did, indeed, draw on a well-established medieval genre. For my purposes, I define universal histories as those medieval histories which take as their subject the theme of salvation history from creation up to the incarnation of Christ (and usually beyond to contemporary events).[3] Universal histories divide this expanse of salvific time into six or seven ages. These ages were then cross-correlated (in ever more complicated ways during the Middle Ages) to an array of genealogies, ranging from the ancestors of Jesus, to relative dates for prophets, emperors, and pontificates. Anna-Dorothee von den Brincken has distinguished three styles (albeit permeable and overlapping) of universal history: the *series temporum*, chiefly concentrating on computation of incarnational years; *mare historiarum*, where moralizing the different ages comes to the fore, especially in those histories written during the Investiture Conflict and the Crusades; and finally *imago mundi*, a strand emphasizing geographical instruction.

From their inception universal histories were conceived as graphic exercises.[4] Scribes used diagrams and schemata to conflate and align the dense information contained in incarnational computation and genealogies. From around 1100, as universal histories grew more graphically complex in an effort to render encyclopedic knowledge of geography, *mappaemundi* began to be used to illustrate the histories. These maps often depicted the holy city of Jerusalem as the center of the world. Like a knot, the Holy City bound together genealogies and time lines and gave them coherency.[5] From the 1470s, printed versions of universal histories began to circulate widely. With each printed edition, they grew more ambitious graphically.[6] Their print layouts exploited the compositional possibilities of woodcuts in order to make time lines (provided by the various genealogical materials) work like slide rules. Just as a slide rule renders linear logarithmic relations, so time lines in these universal histories helped to make linear their spiraling genealogies. Take for example the page layout of the *Fasciculus temporum* by Werner Rolevinck, an incunabulum with over 35 printings between 1474 and 1500. It demonstrates how the time line works as a slide rule[7] (Figure 9). Rolevinck ran parallel time

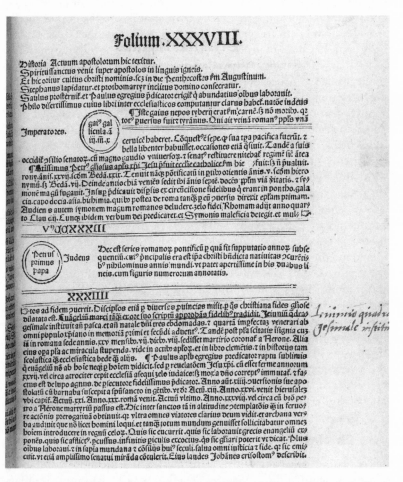

Figure 9. The "slide rule" of universal history. From Werner Rolevinck, *Fasciculus temporum* (Strassburg, 1490), fol. 38r. Courtesy of the Rare Books Division, New York Public Library, Astor, Lennox, and Tilden Foundations.

lines across the center of each page. On one track he marked "Anno Mundi," time from the Creation marked as year 1 and ascending to the current year. On the other track, he indicated time before and after the Incarnation. These years descend from 6666 to the time of the birth of Christ at incarnation year 1 and then begin to ascend to the year of publication. These time lines were cued to genealogies that ran serially throughout the pages of the history. In the prologue Rolevinck described how he imagined his history as a "wall" (*paries*) on which he had "painted" (*depinxi*) "holy scripture and other diverse histories" ("sacrarum scripturarum quam diversarum aliarum historiarum"). The layout should encourage the reader to observe "space and numbers [chronology] as they correspond" ("diligenter obseruet spacia et numerum correspondenter"). These time lines thus worked imaginatively, and not unlike the way in which carbon 14 dating functions, that is, they sought to produce an independent dating device for biblical history. Scholars commonly regard this printed layout as the perfection of a tradition of medieval graphics.[8]

Such graphic perfection is not the only claim of the *Fasciculus temporum* to fame as a universal history; it also inaugurated the popularity of printed universal histories as picture books. Its first two printings in 1474 (Cologne) attracted consumers first with four and then with nine illustrations of city views. The entrepreneurial effort to repackage universal histories as picture books began to cohere in the 1480s. Venetian printers, who controlled almost half of incunabular production in Europe by the midpoint of this decade, ardently promoted illustrations in universal chronicles.[9] By the time of the 1480 Venetian edition of the *Fasciculus*, the number of city views illustrating the text had risen to forty-four. Another best-selling universal history, the popular *Supplementum chronicarum* of Foresti von Bergamo, first published without illustrations in Venice in 1483 and again in 1485, was furnished with woodcuts in the "third edition" of 1486. Bernardinus Benalius, the printer, used a stock of twenty-two woodcuts for seventy-five illustrations in 1486. Over half of these were city views. Such views easily exceeded the number of illustrations with theological subject matter. The *Supplementum chronicarum* issue of 1486 thus almost doubled the number of illustrations featured in its rival.

The Cutting Room Floor

It was within this competitive print market that leading Nuremberg burghers planned the *Nuremberg Chronicle* in 1491. Although scholars insist on the traditional ("medieval") essence of the *Nuremberg Chronicle*, they also remark on its exceptionalism. Its number of city views surpassed those in other competing histories. This incunabulum featured fifty-two different woodcuts of city views dispersed throughout the text. Scholars have grouped the Nuremberg city views into two categories. "Realistic" views (32 examples) bear some kind of detail that distinguished them as the view of a particular city and, unlike imaginary views, they were not reused to illustrate other city views.[10] A strong association exists between these realistic city views and centers for early printing. The realistic views mostly depict towns, usually sites of a bishopric or a university, which had their own printing presses before 1475.[11] There were also blocks of five imaginary city views without distinctive reference to specific cities which were also used only once. In style they are indistinguishable from the "realistic" group. The remaining stock of fourteen woodcuts can be thought of as "generic" views. They differ from each other in detail, but they are not specific to the profile of any "real" city. These generic views could be recycled up to seven times to illustrate the numerous cities being described in the *Chronicle*.

At first glance, the city views that begin to punctuate printed universal histories in the 1480s might seem to disrupt the working of the time line, the graphic slide rule that threads through the universal history and binds it temporally. A closer look, however, suggests otherwise. Let me show what I mean by turning to an analysis of a city view from the *Chronicle*. I take as my example the largest, a full, double-page spread, which depicts none other than Nuremberg itself. The view is set in the section of the universal history devoted to the Sixth Age (Figure 10).[12] Within its graphic folds it encrypts both the historical expulsion of Nuremberg Jews in 1349 and the imaginary displacement of Jerusalem at the knot that binds the temporality of universal history. The geometric center of the woodcut crosses at the spires of the Nuremberg Frauenkirche. Built at the mandate of Emperor Karl IV, this church was constructed on the rubble of the Nuremberg synagogue.[13] At the time of the Black Death the Emperor had ordered the synagogue leveled in order to make way for the development of the Hauptmarkt, a civic development plan that included the construction of the new church. A two-page text praising the town of Nuremberg (100v) elucidates how the displacement of Jerusalem is also at stake in this large woodcut.

The city description structures itself as follows. It rehearses the fame of the city and debates whether it is of Roman or Carolingian origins. Based on the opinions of Aeneas Sylvius Piccolomini (Pius II), it opts for the latter. Some political history then follows, along with a list of Nuremberg churches and monastic communities. The text celebrates the fact that Nuremberg is the repository of the imperial regalia, whose display with accompanying indulgences proved lucrative to the town. At the end of the description of the city a blank space of 4 cm ensues. This gap marks an unusual break for the print layout, which, with almost a *horror vacui*, tends to fill up the surface of the page.[14] After this break the text engages in an impassioned discussion of the "church militant." It emphasizes the importance of Christ as the cornerstone and Peter as the first apostle. The text bemoans those "cheap cousins" who have "planted the Church with teachers, wonders, images, and bloodshed."[15] Turning the page to 101v, the reader finds a full-page woodcut of Christ enthroned with the apostles; the adjoining text on 102r both tells the story of Pentecost and illustrates it with a woodcut. This juxtaposition of the Nuremberg view and the city description with a scene of Pentecost brings us closer to understanding the specific work of the time line in the *Chronicle*. The feast of Pentecost had particular resonance in apocalyptic thinking in the fifteenth century and enjoyed a rich history of illustration.[16] Exegetes

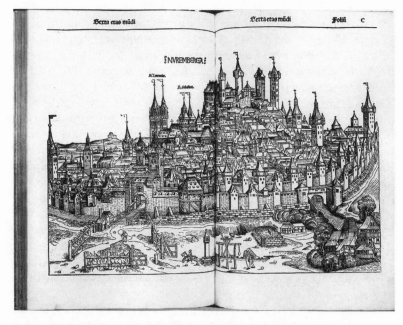

Figure 10. Nuremberg city view. From Hartmann Schedel, *Liber chronicarum* (Nuremberg, 1493), fol. 100r. Courtesy of the Rare Books Division, New York Public Library, Astor, Lennox, and Tilden Foundations.

debated the relation of Pentecost to Christian history. Some regarded church history from the time of Pentecost to the present as crucial to explicating apocalyptic symbols. Some skipped over that history and went from Pentecost straight to the Last Days.[17] At stake in this debate (with all its implications for the Christian typological imaginary) is where to place the hermeneutic divide.

The holy city, which, as we have seen, knotted the universal history as its umbilicus, appears only eccentrically in the *Chronicle's* carefully planned layout. The printers twice used a so-called "realistic" view of Jerusalem to illustrate the story of Solomon (48r) and the destruction of the temple (63v–64r). To illustrate the actual description of Jerusalem, which occurs just before the story of the Flood, the designers chose an "imaginary view." The *Chronicle* thus uses "realism" in the carefully rendered view of Nuremberg, and its central placement in the text, to displace Jerusalem as the spatio-temporal center of universal history.

The *Chronicle's* woodcut of Nuremberg is the earliest known *stand-alone* view of the city. It is not, however, the first known realistic *depiction* of the city. That distinction belongs to a retable painted by Jadolus Kroll in 1483 for the St. Lorenz church in Nuremberg.[18] The distinctive walls and spires of Nuremberg form a backdrop to a scene of the Holy Family. Such carefully delineated city views (and also carefully rendered "landscapes") become typical in Northern painting in the fifteenth century. Art historians usually read this matter as "background," and assume thereby an implicit relation between the theological subject matter of the foreground, such as the Holy Family or the Madonna, and the city view. They mark the birth of secularization and thus the birth of "art history," when such background matter detaches itself from the foreground in order to constitute itself as independent subject matter (the stand-alone city view, or the stand-alone landscape). However, art historian Hans Belting has castigated such linear readings in his thorough analysis of the problems of image and likeness in medieval European art. He shows how such a binary periodization of genre either refuses to recognize, or worse, ignores, the protracted medieval "crisis of the image."[19] Belting argues that only a supersessionary mode of thinking in art history could produce periodization that claims that the so-called history of art begins when city views and landscapes detach themselves from the foreground of traditional theological imagery and come to stand alone, as, for instance, in the *Nuremberg Chronicle.* Instead of such a supersessionary relationship, Belting insists that it is precisely the *discontinuities* of such carefully rendered city views (or landscapes or still lifes) with their theological subjects that make arguments about the crisis of the image internal to the theological representation. Belting asserts that city views work like a citation or a quote within the painting and in so doing they cease to "coexist" seamlessly with theology. In fact, they "cut" theological matter.

As artists cut the block for the Nuremberg city view, they excised the theological subject matter that was still to be seen on display in the Kroll altarpiece.[20] Images of the Holy Family or the Madonna, once attached to the city view, along with the central image of Jerusalem, lay on the cutting room floor of the Koberger print shop. Just as the city views of the *Nuremberg Chronicle* cut out theological subjects, so did its universal history qua universal history cut out Jerusalem from the center, the nodal point that threaded together the temporality of medieval Christian salvation history. The question becomes: what difference did this make for the typological imaginary?

The printed advertisement for the *Chronicle* hinted at an answer when it promised its readers "so great delight in reading it that you will think you are not reading a series of stories, but looking at them with your own eyes."[21] A moving picture before the invention of moving pictures, the *Chronicle* made it possible to see time in a new way. The city views (especially that of Nuremberg) translated time into place; they acted as the coordinates of this translation process—thus their graphic centrality in the *Nuremberg Chronicle*.[22] The syncopation of city views throughout the universal history had the effect of excising Jerusalem from its nodal graphic point in salvific time. In doing so, city views also "cut out" the long-standing hermeneutic divide between the Old Testament and the New Testament. The city views graphically reoccupied the typological imaginary of Jerusalem. They are not thus simply "secularizing" Jerusalem, as some scholars would have it. Instead, I argue, they are taking new graphic representations of urban space (city views) and typologizing them. As readers relinked theological time to this new hermeneutic divide, they would have to typologize themselves as readers, just as the graphics typologized city views. They would come to imagine themselves as the faithful synagogue located in their newly typologized urban imaginary. The new reader would then fashion herself as a "type" of an old Christian self whose links between time and space came preconstituted in the long history of the redemptive holy image. A self portrait (1500) by Albrecht Dürer, another Nuremberg artist involved in the production of the *Chronicle,* is an example of the kind of typologized "subject" I am imagining reading the Nuremberg city view.[23] The reader herself becomes a typologized citation of the living icon (Figure 11).

Colligite Fragmenta Ne Pereant

Collect the fragments lest they perish.[24]

This chapter could stop here at the analysis of the layers of scar tissue accreting around the void created around the central place of Jerusalem excised in the *Nuremberg Chronicle*. Recall the first cut— there was the rubble produced by leveling the Jewish neighborhood to make way for a new marketplace. Over the foundations of the synagogue Nuremberg burghers built the Frauenkirche, the church that constituted the geometric center of the city view of Nuremberg as centerpiece of the *Chronicle*. Another cut—the syncopated city views cut out Jerusalem as the navel of universal history. The graphic work of the secret room of the Koberger print shop thus not only synchronized a series of spatial strategies, it also performed the synthetic work of abstract substitution of new forms of representation of urban space for the typological imaginary of Jerusalem.[25] The Nuremberg city view presses us to think about spatio-temporal circuits of gain and loss at work in its layers of substitutions. Julia Lupton has insisted on the importance of studying the circuits of loss and gain in the typological imaginary:

From the perspective of survival, we need to correct the periodic retransactions carried out at the cataclysmic junctures of Western history by heeding those foreign elements made foreign precisely by the fact of persisting beyond the moment of their historic supercedure.[26]

I want to propose as a missing link in the circuit of loss and gain in the *Nuremberg Chronicle* none other than Hartmann Schedel, its editor. He is the silent partner in the printing project who goes unmentioned in the archive of its contractual exchanges. We know from the preserved manuscript exemplar, used as the layout for the Latin version of the *Chronicle*, that Schedel painstakingly wrote out most of the text himself. Schedel, counted as a member of the circle of early German humanists, had studied at Leipzig and Padua. He returned to Nuremberg in 1480, where he practiced medicine until his death in 1514. He left behind a library, which contained over 370 manuscripts and 600 printed titles. He collected widely in Italian humanism: Vitruvius, Alberti, Petrarch, and Ficino, for example. He possessed a copy of Tacitus's *Germania* and of course a canon of classical authors. He owned the latest works in universal history such as the *Fasciculus*

Figure 11. Albrecht Dürer (1471–1528), *Self-Portrait*, 1500. Alte Pinakothek, Munich. Courtesy of Foto Marburg/Art Resource, New York.

temporum, as well as newly printed titles in geography, including Ptolemy's *Geographia.* Also represented in his personal library were rich collections in medicine, surgery, law, math, theology, and devotion.[27]

It is through the notebooks of Schedel, in particular, that we are able to link this stereotype of a German humanist with the circuit of survival and loss circulating in Koberger's secret room. One such notebook, copied in 1504, is illuminating. It includes an array of topical humanist material, such as the first known sylloge of Etruscan inscriptions, drawings of ancient sarcophagi and inscriptions from Rome, literary pieces such as a copy of Annius of Viterbo's *Borgiana Lucubratio,* and a version of the poem *Antichità Prospettiche Romane.* Schedel also jotted down in the same notebook some deeply sexualized anti-Italian epigrams composed at a bacchanalian meeting of German humanists which took place in Regensburg in November 1493, just four months after the appearance of the Latin version of the *Nuremberg Chronicle.* The poems are obsessed with depicting Italian humanists as pederasts and sodomites. As one poem puts it: Germans "bang beavers" ("futuisse cunnos") and Italians "fuck butts" ("culos futire").[28] These poems sexualize the boundaries of competitive ethnonationalist humanist circles. They rehearse deeply felt tensions among humanists regarding the fashioning of nationalism, sexuality, and antiquarianism at stake in collecting literary fragments. These jottings help us read the *Nuremberg Chronicle* against the grain of current scholarship, which insists, as I have already mentioned, on its medieval exemplarity. Schedel's literary fragments help us to understand how the surgery in the secret room was a kind of plastic surgery. As these Nuremberg burghers excised Jerusalem, they produced Nuremberg around that void, imagined as the safely heterosexual civic site of a new, intellectual nationalism.[29]

The burghers also initiated a purification process as they phantasmatically substituted Nuremberg for Jerusalem and architecturally and graphically reoccupied the Nuremberg synagogue with the Frauenkirche. The *Chronicle* helped to cut out contemporary Jews who had hitherto been ostensibly protected in the typological imaginary as a typological relic. The surgery undertaken in Koberger's secret room threw contemporary Nuremberg Jews phantasmatically into a kind of "free-fall."[30] In amputating theological subject matter from the representation of the city view and by relocating Nuremberg as the node of universal history, city views "expelled" contemporary Jews not only from space but also from typological time. By severing the links of the typological imaginary and reconnecting those links within the Old Testament (rather than between the Old and New Testaments), Nuremberg burghers no longer needed Jews to guarantee the apocalyptic teleology of universal history. In a sense the Apocalypse was now already and not yet, that is "simul" with the substitution of the Christian faithful synagogue for the pre-Diasporan Jews of the Hebrew Scriptures (*veritas hebraica*).[31] The Nuremberg Jews among whom they lived, the "Talmud Jews" imagined as a false species of Jews who could guarantee nothing, became the detritus of universal history. Shortly after the publication of the *Nuremberg Chronicle* and just three years before their expulsion (1498) from Nuremberg, Conrad Celtis, humanist laureate, wrote that no city in Germany was immune from the contumely of the Jews who stole hosts and polluted the Eucharist.[32] Resident Jews would be forced to leave Nuremberg (again) in 1498, not to return until 1850.

The same circle of Nuremberg printers and artists involved in the *Chronicle* also served as members of the town council, as it petitioned the Emperor for permission to expel the Jews. They also partook in Nuremberg civic festivals which included the antisemitic performances and publications of Hans Folz.[33] The graphic dispossession of Jews was intertwined with an array of legal and civic strategies directed at the reoccupation of things Jewish. Consider these three exemplary anecdotes. When the Emperor Maximilian gave permission for the eviction of the Jews from Nuremberg in 1498, the City Council acquired their abandoned houses. Anton Koberger presented one of these houses as a dowry for his daughter in 1500. In his collection of woodcuts and engravings, Hartmann Schedel, the *Chronicle*'s "editor," pasted several of his collected prints onto parchment leaves that had been torn from a late medieval Hebrew manuscript sent to him by a Dominican friend upon the expulsion of the Jews from Bamberg. Finally, Albrecht Altdorfer—a contemporary of Koberger, Schedel, and Dürer—who, like the latter, worked for Emperor Maximilian, and who served as an important member of town government in Regensburg, etched (February 1519) two haunting views of the porch and interior of the Regensburg synagogue upon the expulsion of the Jews from that town.[34] A voyeuristic fascination with textual, graphic, and architectural spaces emptied of Jews haunts these stories. That fascination, I would argue, draws its energy from relocating the hermeneutic divide of the typological imaginary in order to render imaginable the reoccupation of the Old Testament by the faithful synagogue of the Christians.[35]

Ethnography and City Views

The act of collection is a means of protecting objects from the taint of dynamic temporal processes. Collection relies on synchronicity as a way of producing the space of collection as an effect. Thus, we should not be surprised to find the so-called "early modern" museum collection accreting around the cut made by city views into the temporal imaginary of the medieval universal histories. Collections of city views, which began to circulate in Europe in the mid-sixteenth century as stand-alone graphic artifacts collectible in so-called "modern atlases,"[36] trace further how such typological sundering, under discussion in this chapter, worked as a graphic practice. Their force can be grasped by a comparison. Consider, for example, another city view of Nuremberg engraved for the 1575 edition of *Civitates orbis terrarum* printed by Georg Braun and Franz Hogenberg (1572–1618) (Figure 12).

When readers bought a copy of volume two of *Civitates orbis terrarum*, they could turn to page 43 for the view of Nuremberg. There they found a 50 line description of the city backed by a two-page engraved view.[37] No mention is made of the religious confession of Nuremberg (no sense in discouraging sales across Catholic and Protestant audiences). The account praises the industry of its inhabitants. The view itself (22.5 × 34.5 cm) differs markedly from the 1493 view in its handling of the space before the walls. The view allows for proportionately more "foreground" and peoples it in a way that the

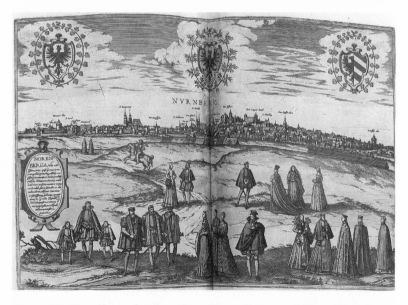

Figure 12. Nuremberg city view. From Georg Braun and Franz Hogenberg, *Civitates orbis terrarum* (1575). By permission of the Newberry Library, Chicago.

earlier view did not. Starting with the lower right foreground, the reader sees four views of different stages of formal dress and hairstyle of a richly clad young woman. The front, side, and back views emphasize details such as the fall of fabric, the border designs of hems, and the braiding of hair. Another woman (a servant?) also in this group is depicted in simpler dress. She holds a basket, a stem of flowers, and a vase with flowers. Behind this grouping, poses yet another group consisting of a mustached man sporting a sword and an elegantly clad woman attended by two young women. Again the reader is invited to linger on the carefully delineated textures of the textiles used in clothing the women as well as the "architecture" of trains and tubular hats. Moving along the foreground the reader encounters further a mixed group of two women and a man, each elaborately dressed; a group of three elegantly dressed, bearded "city-fathers" carrying swords; an elegantly dressed man with (presumably) his two young sons, whose hands he holds. As the reader's eyes scan the center ground they behold a man with feathers in his cap talking to a simply clad woman with a basket under her arm. A mounted horseman rides in the mid-distance. Finally two women with their backs to the reader stand in the far foreground, just across from the walls of Nuremberg.

This Nuremberg view from the *Civitates orbis terrarum* maps in its foreground what I want to call a "local ethnography," that is, a "collection" of various views and perspectives on local aspects of gender, age, class, dress, fabric, hair. Sartorial in its emphasis, this ethnography recalls the sumptuary concerns of sixteenth-century urban law. The Nuremberg city walls have become the backdrop to its local ethnography which has displaced the city wall far back into the view. The suturing of the ethnographic foreground to the background of the city view renders the foreground figures proportionately as big as city walls.

The 1575 view in *Civitates orbis terrarum* brings the 1493 woodcut of Nuremberg full circle. Figures have reestablished themselves in the foreground of an early-modern city view. They return as ethnographic subjects, that is, as a catalog or collection. Their appearance suggests crucial links between the reoccupation of the Old Testament by the Christian faithful synagogue (the graphic work of the *Nuremberg Chronicle*) and the emergence of the disciplinary practice of early modern ethnography. Where once Jews were considered relics when the hermeneutic divide rested between the Old Testament and the New, now the Christian body itself emerges as a graphic spatial effect, a collection, at the new hermeneutical divide. I am not rendering these two moments equivalent, nor am I saying that some ahistorical antisemitism is at stake in this early-modern city view. Instead, I am trying to historicize the Christian cultural imaginary at whose core lies a relation to Judaism. I am trying to tell a story of discontinuities within repetition, or repetition with a difference of the typological imaginary. My account of the city views of Nuremberg tells a tale of crisis in the Christian typological imaginary resolved graphically by excision of a traditional theological subject from the space of the medieval image. From the voided space of the foreground gradually emerged a new, ethnographic subject, a subject which is spatial and frozen in empty time. Enter the collection.[38] Enter what Julia Reinhard Lupton has cogently described as "the crafting of myths of modernity precisely out of the religious material that formed such an important part of [their] early modern daily vocabularies."[39] Regard the collection as the afterlife of medieval universal history to be haunted by its evocation of Jews as that which is unconscious to Christianity,[40] that is, "what remains radically repressed by and hence disturbingly internal to it, the imploded husk of a previous representational system."[41]

Chapter 3
Graphic Reoccupation, the Faithful Synagogue, and Foucault's Genealogy

Corpus Mysticum Becoming Fidelis Synagoga

A view and description of the town of Regensburg (Figure 13) opens the Sixth Age of the *Nuremberg Chronicle*, which age, recall, featured the city of Nuremberg as its centerpiece. At the time that artists cut the woodblock for Regensburg, its Jewish inhabitants numbered around 500, estimated one of the largest urban Jewish populations in late medieval Germany. Unlike the historic Jewish quarter in Nuremberg which had been leveled at the time of the Black Death, that of Regensburg still occupied its traditional area south of the Cathedral Square when the *Chronicle* was being compiled. Walls enclosed the Judenstadt (as the burghers called it), an area covering over 14,000 square meters, in which could be found over thirty houses, community schools, and a synagogue whose construction dated back to a period of building after the First Crusade. Yet no graphic trace of this substantial Jewish neighborhood can be found in the *Chronicle* woodcut depicting the city.

What did not materialize graphically in 1493 would take graphic form in February 1519. At that time burghers of Regensburg ordered the destruction of the synagogue and the expulsion of its resident Jews. My first encounter with two etchings (Figures 14, 15) executed by Albrecht Altdorfer, who recorded the Regensburg synagogue immediately prior to the destruction, chilled me. I found them reproduced in a study of Altdorfer's landscapes; they can also be found in compendia of early Renaissance etchings and engravings, and in catalogues of Altdorfer's work. Genre, medium, oeuvre—none of these categories suffices to provide a reading practice capable of addressing the gap between these two images. It is between the one study of two

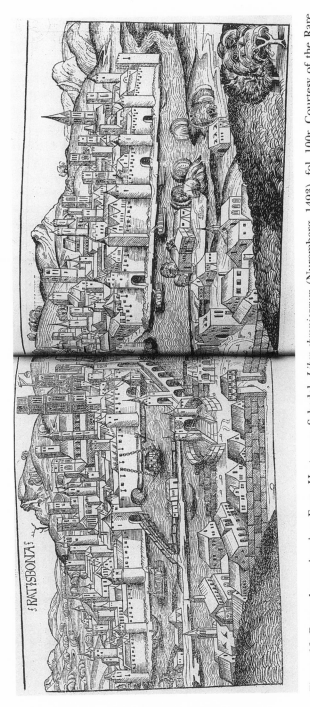

Figure 13. Regensburg city view. From Hartmann Schedel, *Liber chronicarum* (Nuremberg, 1493), fol. 100r. Courtesy of the Rare Books Division, New York Public Library, Astor, Lennox, and Tilden Foundations.

Jews standing on the threshold of the Regensburg synagogue (Figure 14) and the second of its architectural interior (stripped of liturgical furniture) that graphic technologies do the work of the typological imaginary. How can we read the temporal interval of this graphic project that transformed a representation of Jews, coeval with Altdorfer, into a rendering of interior architectural space? Put another way: how does the Jew, long regarded by Christians as a typological shadow (umbra), get reduced to a cluster of shadowy hatchings incised onto a copper plate in order to fabricate spatial perspective? How does such a reduction, as repetition of the crisis of the Christian typological imaginary, hatch out the emergence of the space of the aesthetic? We can almost overhear Dürer musing: "Waß aber dy schonheit seÿ, daz weis jch nit" ("What beauty is, I do not know").[1] The space of the aesthetic becomes a crypt for the expelled Jews of Regensburg.

What I want to do in this chapter is to wrench these etchings out of the too familiar aesthetic categories of genre, medium, and oeuvre and relocate them in a history of the Christian typological imaginary with its crises of repetition. As we have learned so far, in the twelfth century the new graphic technologies of the modular page gridded the biblical text in textbooks and rendered it an image. In so doing such graphic technologies paradoxically voided the text. The central space of the page devoted to representation of the text became a ruin at which site systems of stereotypical typological illustration flourished. In the fifteenth century graphic techniques, such as etching and engraving, newly linked to printing technologies, fabricated a new kind of surface—the rendering of abstract architectural space, on which Christians could phantasmatically enact the reoccupation of the Old Testament as members of the faithful synagogue (*fidelis synagoga*).[2] As the Altdorfer etchings move the viewer from the porch of the synagogue into its denuded interior, they graphically perform the act of reoccupation that is the subject of both the *Chronicle* and these etchings. Such reoccupation deserves our attention for its anxious efforts (once again) to reground the typological imaginary. Where once circumcision of the heart had superseded the cut of the foreskin, Christians were now superseding the mystical body of Christ with the *fidelis synagoga*. Remember that the typological imaginary was founded "upon the *loss of a body*—the loss of the body of Jesus Christ, compounded with the loss of the 'body' of Israel, of a 'nation' and its genealogy."[3] Once graphic projects such as the *Nuremberg Chronicle* drop out coeval Jews as a term in this repetition of loss, one finds only their shadowy traces subsequently encoded in the graphic hatching of Altdorfer's etchings. Perhaps some readers might wish to construe the reoccupation of the *fidelis synagoga* by the *corpus mysticum* positively as

Figure 14. Albrecht Altdorfer, Porch of the Regensburg Synagogue, 1519. Berlin, Kupferstichkabinett. Photo courtesy of Bildarchiv Preussischer Kulturbesitz.

Figure 15. Albrecht Altdorfer, Interior of the Regensburg Synagogue, 1519. Berlin, Kupferstichkabinett. Photo courtesy of Bildarchiv Preussischer Kulturbesitz.

repetition with a difference, a performance that would open the typological imaginary up to other possibilities. Instead, I argue that the Altdorfer etchings give us a disturbing example of repetition as foreclosure. Such foreclosure traumatically encrypts Jews within the tomb of the typological imaginary at the same time that it fabricates a writing surface constitutive of a new graphic regime of "scientific" representation. An analysis of such representational strategies can help us to rethink Christian-Jewish relations not as something incomprehensible, instinctive, ahistorical, but rather as a graphic genealogy of the mechanical power of the "rational" and the "technical" in the typological imaginary.[4]

Clues to the technologies of the typological imaginary abound in the etchings, in each of which Altdorfer incorporated an epigraphic plaque. The first inscription reads: PORTICUS SINAGOGAE / IUDAICAE RATISPONEN[SIS] / FRACTA 21 DIE FEB. / ANN. 1519 (The porch of the Jewish synagogue at Regensburg destroyed February 21, 1519). The second reads: ANNO D[OMI]NI D XIX / IUDAICA RATISPONA / SYNAGOGA IUSTO / DEI IUDICIO FUNDIT[U]S EST EVERSA (in the year of the Lord 1519 the Jewish Regensburg synagogue was utterly destroyed by the just judgment of God). The language of the second epigraph in particular struck me. I knew that the formula, "iusto dei iudicio" ("by the just judgment of God"), came from the juridical world of the medieval ordeal. By ordeal I mean a medieval method of trial in which the accused was exposed to a physical test, such as hot iron or boiling water applied to the flesh, from which he or she, if innocent, would be protected by God.[5] The rendering of the interior of the synagogue also draws on the rich architectural metaphors developed by Christians for discussing circumcision. I knew from my readings of medieval anti-Jewish polemic that the repudiation of circumcision under the New Law, its effacement as an inscription, was imagined in architectural terms. The epigraph's claim "funditus est eversa" ("was utterly destroyed") hauntingly echoes traditional commentary on Isaiah 28:16 to be found in anti-Jewish polemic, such as the *Disputatio* by Gilbert Crispin, who compares Christ to the cornerstone of the temple of Sion. As a *carefully hewn* cornerstone Christ "justifies circumcision from the faith and the foreskin through the faith" ("circumcisionem iustificat ex fide et preputium per fidem").[6] Altdorfer's epigraphic gesture, the public lettering of the plaques in each print, also pointed to the importance of transmitting a message as civic and monumental knowledge. Together, these clues suggested to me that the prints worked as a montage condensing the juridical world of the ordeal, the ritual of circumcision, and the work of public writing. To read against the typological imaginary would entail unfolding these various superimpositions. By the end of the chapter, I hope to open the crypt etched by Altdorfer and then refold the etchings like a paper sculpture to show how they work: fold the porch of the synagogue (Figure 14) to become the lining of a crypt and then roll out the second etching (Figure 15) to become the slab to be placed over that crypt. The typological imaginary used this slab as both a new graphic surface and a new epistemological surface out of which the problem of the aesthetic would be fabricated.

The Duel over Inscription

The foreskin is the first clue. Beginning in late antiquity, who was circumcised and who was not came to play a crucial role in differentiating Christians from Jews theologically.[7] My reading of the Altdorfer etchings begins, then, with the rites of baptism and circumcision and how these rites came to confer theological status by virtue of their differentiating inscriptions. Richly discursive and passionately held differences over pleasure, sexual renunciation, and the hierarchy of body and soul came to be polarized in early Christianity around the heart in baptism and the foreskin in circumcision. Since a graphic struggle over the legibility of these two modes of cutting and inscribing marked a divide from late antiquity, and since the architectural content of the Altdorfer etchings proposes an afterlife of this struggle, I am approaching the cultural politics of such struggles as a contest over graphic technologies.

Rites of baptism and circumcision do not occur in isolation. They are performances of embodiment that take place within wider institutional settings in which markings are interpreted for their visibility and legibility. Institutions also have their own graphic processes, their own writing machines. A study of conflict over these inscriptions, therefore, requires a notion of inscription that can account for how a graphic scripted on the body or soul can travel from that body or soul into institutional networks. Cultural studies of scientific representation, in particular of inscription, offer a way of thinking about such leaps.

Bruno Latour, a sociologist of science, thinks of inscription as the graphic transformation of things in the world, visible and invisible, such as stars, viruses, genes, bodies, and so on, onto paper (and now onto disk) for the purposes of dissemination. Thus, for example, some aspect of dinosaur locomotion can be graphically rendered and that rendering can be photographed or digitally scanned. The image can then be reproduced in a variety of formats, such as museum exhibits, books, slides, films, videos, tee-shirts, which can in turn be disseminated and travel. These traveling inscriptions can be seen and recognized by thousands of viewers and can conscript them into believing in the validity of a particular representation of dinosaurs (say, the kinder, gentler, smarter mammalian dinosaur), a beast, which, after all, no one has actually seen alive. Inscriptions, according to Latour, thus "allow conscriptions" of viewers around representation and are therefore powerful mobilizing tools.[8]

Like the initial artistic rendering of the dinosaur, medieval anti-Jewish polemics (mostly fictionalized Christian accounts of disputes between Christian and Jewish intellectuals) can be regarded as graphic transformations of the invisible inscription of baptism on the heart and the visible inscription of circumcision on the foreskin into monastic and university networks where disputes over ethnic legibility were further engaged. Some further discussion of two of the most popular medieval Christian-Jewish disputations, namely Petrus Alfonsi's *Dialogi contra Iudaeos* (1108–10) and Gilbert Crispin's *Disputatio Iudaei et Christiani* (ca. 1096)—already introduced in Chapter 1— shows how such translations operate to construct networks of inscriptions organized around conflicts over the legibility of baptism and circumcision.[9]

In the prologue to Crispin's *Disputatio*, the reader learns the outcome of the debate between the Christian and the Jew, its "happy ending"—the Jewish interlocutor is baptized in a public ceremony in London and becomes a monk. The very writing of this *Disputatio*, then, constitutes a graphic inscription of baptism onto the textual body of the Jewish interlocutor. Imagine that Crispin writes his text on the heart of his Jewish interlocutor as a way of making the inscription of baptism visible. Whereas Crispin, as a Christian, works out the problem of baptism for Jews, Petrus Alfonsi, as a baptized Jew, works out the problem of both baptism and circumcision in his *Dialogi*, disputing with his former Jewish self, which he enfolds in the persona of Moses. As we have seen in Chapter 1, he uses scientific arguments and—importantly, for the first time in this polemical genre—scientific diagrams, in order to discredit Moses and his talmudic knowledge for their irrationality.[10] These diagrams are not merely scientific inscriptions; they also work to cover over Alfonsi's circumcision. Alfonsi inscribes these scientific diagrams like tattoos over the visible "writing" of his circumcision, thereby rendering circumcision an illegible inscription that cannot be linked to "science." Scientific diagrams render visible the invisible graphic of his baptism.

Alfonsi's strategy of using diagram and text linked his polemic not only into theological networks but into "scientific" ones as well, in which scholars explored new work in astronomy and astrology. Graphic contests thus traveled to new audiences. Not surprisingly, his polemic was one of the most widely disseminated of this medieval genre precisely because it combined sought-after scientific diagrams with polemic over ethnic inscription. In contrast, the Crispin *Disputatio* contains no diagrams. It matched the popularity of the Alfonsi text in the twelfth century (with a total of twenty-two extant manuscripts), but then interest tailed off quickly with only seven copies extant in the thirteenth century and only two copies in the fourteenth and fifteenth centuries. It would seem that the lack of diagrams in Crispin's *Disputatio* constrained its circulation to a narrower temporal and pietistic network and thereby dampened its effect.

So far I have tried to show how the genre of anti-Jewish polemic came to translate a Christian conflict over corporeal inscription into graphic forms that, as a mobilizing tool, could circulate widely beyond any one body, thus significantly expanding the discursive field. There were, however, important inscriptional limits to how long the chain of translation could become in twelfth-century Christendom. The dead end lay with the all-important link to the juridical writing machine of the day, the ordeal. This was a form of proof which relied on hot water, hot irons, or immersion to determine the guilt or innocence of the accused in cases where normal juridical procedures, most notably compurgation (the sworn endorsement of friends and neighbors of the accused), were not deemed applicable.

The second plaque of the Altdorfer etching superimposes the juridical language of the ordeal onto the empty, stripped space of the interior of the Regensburg synagogue. The epigraphy, its chiseled quality, insistently reminds that inscription played a crucial role in the ordeal. The blistering impact of hot water or hot iron "inscribed" the hand of the accused with signs to be read and interpreted for guilt or innocence. The chief ritual parallel for the ordeal was baptism; indeed, in Old Norse the words for ordeal and baptism are the same. The limitation of the ordeal, however, lay in its inability to translate the wound or scar of the hot water or iron into a graphic that could be disseminated more widely in inscriptional networks. The ordeal could only inscribe the flesh; it did not produce a disseminating inscription in the form of parchment. Just as Crispin's *Disputatio* was limited to the ritual performance of the baptism of the Jewish interlocutor in London, so its corporeal writing pad confined the ordeal. These graphic limitations traced a historical perimeter to the discursive field of graphic conflict.

By fiat of the prelates gathered at the Fourth Lateran Council, convened in 1215, the inquest came to reoccupy the juridical process of ordeal.[11] Whereas in the ordeal hot iron or hot water "wrote" the corporeal inscription, in the inquest the main graphic gesture was notarial. A notary was always present to commit the oral proceedings to parchment or later to paper, thus producing an official record (written most often in Latin before 1450). The inquest thus breached the perimeters of dissemination hitherto set by the ordeal. Put another way, inquisitorial process *translated* the corporeal writing pad of the ordeal into the trial record, which was a portable graphic that could be extracted, stored, copied, and circulated.

The practice of the inquest became the core of the process that historians have dubbed as *inquisition.* The graphic practice of inquisition multiplied the possibilities of translation and thus extended the chain of the inscriptional network; it thus transformed and intensified the conflict over inscription between Christians and Jews. Also key to understanding this reframing of inscriptional conflict is medieval torture, the threat of which was necessary to inquisition, and the practice of which predictably accompanied its spread. Torture raises the important question of the relation of the textual bodies produced by the notary's writing hand and the sentient bodies that might endure the pain of torture. Is the tortured body to be thought of as the body of the ordeal displaced by the notarial writing hand? This question, I think, is also relevant to reading the Altdorfer etchings. Are the Jews in the porch of the synagogue in the first etching to be thought of as the body of the ordeal (to which the plaque of the second etching refers) displaced by the etching hand of Altdorfer?

The answer to this question is no, since the question misunderstands the typological imaginary and its graphic processes. Inquisitorial writing produced textual bodies in a writing space that works like a montage, in which different and discontinuous spaces exist simultaneously and collide. If we think of the notorious O. J. Simpson trial of 1995, we know that the trial witnessed by the jury was very different from the trial witnessed by television viewers. We might say that the jury occupied a different, noncontinuous space literally and conceptually. Similarly, the space in which inquisitorial writing took place, conceptually speaking, was different and discontinuous from the space of both the accused and the tortured. There is no unity of gesture and situation in the inquisitorial writing space. These disjunctures, this issue of montage, sharply question the traditional ways in which medieval historians have read and interpreted inquisitorial trial transcripts and should enhance our understanding of how inquisitions inscribed and disseminated the inscription of baptism in the Christian-Jewish competition over legibility.

Two inquisition cases will show how the inquisitorial writing space worked and also how the gesture of inquisitorial writing actually produced the graphic of ritual during the course of these trials.[12] First, take the famous trial in 1320 of Baruch, a noted rabbi, in the court of Jacques Fournier, bishop of Pamiers, the future Pope Benedict XII. This inquisition revolved around the question of whether Baruch's baptism under the threat of death at the hands of marauding Pastorelli was authentic or forced. Without the trial the status of Baruch's baptism would remain in question, illegible. The question then is one of inscription. How can an inquisition decide legibility?

The bishop draws up the sides in this inquisition. He insists, in outright contradiction of Baruch's confession, that there was no absolute force (*coactione absoluta*) involved in his baptism; therefore Baruch is obliged by law and reason (*secundem iura et racionem*) to concur in his baptism; otherwise the bishop will proceed against him as an obstinate heretic. An uncanny, elliptical disjuncture then ensues in the trial record. At this point the different and noncontinuous spaces of the inquest collide as the bishop engages Baruch in a lengthy disputation, similar in genre to the polemic of Alfonsi and Crispin. The collision, however, transforms the disputation from a polemic to a trial by battle. Here we have a montage that produces the bishop and Baruch as armed contestants ready for ordeal by combat. In the gap between the writing space and the accused, the ritual of the duel over inscription takes place.

To make a long disputation short, Baruch "loses" the judicial combat. He then swears that the persecution that resulted in his baptism was for the good of his soul; he now believes from the heart. The bishop "wins" the efficacy of the trial record to render legible the inscription of baptism on the heart of Baruch. If one wanted to find graphic evidence of Baruch's baptism, one would revert not to his body but to the trial record. The inquisition produced illegible or invisible inscriptions as visible and legible graphics that then resided in archived inquisitorial registers, which could and did travel. This is the graphic fantasy of the typological imaginary.

Graphic Doubles

Trial records were not only handwritten; after 1450 extracts and versions of trial records could be disseminated rapidly in print. Remember, too, that Altdorfer, who worked in a variety of print and nonprint media, chose etching, a print medium, for his renderings of the Regensburg synagogue. Did print technology refigure yet again the inscriptional conflict between Christian and Jews? The Trent ritual-murder trial of 1475 offers an important example of graphic overlapping of inquisition with print culture. The trial record, con-structed from the torture and interrogation of nineteen Trent Jews, eighteen men and one woman, narrates the details of an alleged ritual murder, including bleeding, mutilation, and circumcision, of a Chris-tian child named Simon (Figure 8). This print is just one example of the printed images that circulated along with printed as well as hand-written versions of the Trent trial record. It depicts, in the crowded and seemingly medicalized space of the medieval barber, the body of a little male Christian patient/victim spread out on a table. Jewish bar-ber/torturers pinch his flesh, draw his blood, and circumcise him. This engraving offers important evidence of yet another layer of trans-lation of inscriptional conflict, a translation from the torture cham-ber to the world of the reader of printed books and collector of "holy images."

The relays of this translation from torture chamber to printed image are worth pausing over. In the torture chamber at Trent, Chris-tians tortured Jews. In the engraving, Jews become torturers; one brandishes the knife of circumcision. Their victim is a Christian. The tortured bodies of the Jews of Trent are translated by the illustrator into the graphic body of Simon Martyr; the graph of their circumci-sion inscribes itself onto the little boy's body, just as the hot water and hot iron of the ordeal inscribed itself on the accused. The engraving turns both the sacrament of baptism and the torture room inside out. The proliferation of woodcuts and engravings depicting the Trent trial and the boy martyr Simon extended the writing space of the in-quisition into the reading space of the viewer; montage is becoming more encompassing, enchaining.

The violence of the Simon images, their *double graphic* of a baptized boy being circumcised, tells us about the terror of Christians at their own violence/pleasure. The fantastical scene tells about what I have called the "binding" work of fantasy. Rather than think about the trau-matic historical loss at stake in encounters with Jews, these fantasy scenes invented by Christians were a way of managing the fantasy as a kind of pleasure that discharges the trauma as a kind of repetition compulsion.[13] Such inquisitions are not really about "knowledge" but about pleasure, a pleasure that denies its violence and claims it as knowledge. Pleasure and knowledge of inquisition collapse into each other in the Trent engraving and make it impossible to acknowledge "the other's defiance, which is of what encounter consists."[14] With the Trent engraving, as in the Altdorfer etchings, the typological imagi-nary teeters on the edge of ethnography, where the fantasy of the ontological absence of coeval Jews becomes a new writing surface.[15]

We have seen that ecclesiastical inquisition, as a writing machine, multiplied the graphic sites of contest over Christian-Jewish inscription, since the inscribed bodies produced by inquisition could be reproduced in other media and disseminated even more widely. The inquisition thus extended the possibilities for chains of inscriptions, ever broadening the discursive field of graphic conflict. The inquisitorial writing machine worked as a graphic apparatus for performing ritual at a distance, something we have seen that the ordeal could not do.

What does this have to do with repetition and the typological imaginary? To ponder this question further, I would now like to return to the Altdorfer etchings in order to ask whether printing itself had become constitutive of the typological imaginary by the end of the fifteenth century. The Altdorfer etchings teach us the strength to be found in conscription through inscription. Altdorfer translates the expelled Jews of his city into the hatchings of architectural space. Their absence in the second etching becomes the formal presence of "perspectival" architecture. This translation marks an important shift in register in the typological imaginary. It graphs the act of foreclosure in the typological imaginary at which Jews are reduced to an ontological absence. Altdorfer's very act of etching architectural space, rendering the synagogue as an architectural study, becomes constitutive of a new "modern" discourse, ethnography. The architectural space etched by Altdorfer forecloses further conflict over circumcision between Christians and Jews. In so doing, the etching effaces the inscription of circumcision—violent pleasure has become the "knowledge" of space itself. Architectural rendering as a new category of representation covers over the cut foreskin and becomes a fantastical means for Christians of binding and regulating the threatening encounter with neighboring Jews. The typological imaginary occupies the site of "science" in its becoming "ethnography."

The etchings produce something new in the temporal imaginary— a crypt. It is on that surface that the ethnographer Altdorfer signs his monogram. His ethnography is no longer about contested co-presence of Jews with Christians, but, rather, the narcissism of the Same; the etchings resolve the abiding conflict over legibility. Early modern ethnography has traveled to the world of empty chronology. I argue then that the bodily inscriptions of baptism and circumcision and the cascades of graphic translations which passed through such diverse media as polemic, torture chambers, engravings, and etchings came to constitute Christian-Jewish relations at the level of the printed graphic itself. By implication I am saying that printing not only represented this contest but actually came to constitute it. As such, graphic inscriptions signifying conflict between Christian and Jews linked together cascades of discursive networks. Altdorfer's architectural translation might then be read not only as the new writing surface of ethnography but also as the crypt in which Christians finally buried the foreskin, thus foreclosing the possibility of mourning the loss of corporeal inscription which Paul had disavowed so many centuries earlier.

Genealogy, Nature, History

This crypt, its graphic materiality, works as the timepiece of periodization. Its staunch resistance to recent critiques of periodization should give us pause. A case in point can be found in the work of Michel Foucault, whose efforts to refigure periodization foundered too, I argue, on the typological imaginary. In his essay, "Nietzsche, Genealogy, History," Foucault imagined a new form of history, which he termed genealogical history or "effective" history. He imagined genealogy as the "transformation of history into a totally different form of time."[16] He eschewed "traditional history" whose temporality is identitary time, that is time "closed upon itself" and one with itself.[17] Foucault observed that traditional historians divide their continuous time lines with the arbitrary binary of "that was then" and "this is now." The "now" supersedes the "then." Foucault held that genealogical history, by the sheer force of its opposition to "traditional history," could uproot "its traditional foundations and relentlessly disrupt its pretended continuity."[18] He believed that his genealogical practice could disrupt, even stop, the return of the "eunuchs of history" (traditional historians) whom he, like his muse Nietzsche, despised.[19] Foucault's genealogical method does indeed attempt to denature traditional history, yet, paradoxically, the trope of castration—his fascination with eunuchs—inadvertently produces genealogical history as the always already coherent field not subject to lack. Presumably the foreskin and the testicles are intact in the fantasy of genealogical history! He subsequently repeated the image of the eunuch at a crucial moment in the *History of Sexuality*: "Let us not picture the bourgeoisie symbolically castrating itself the better to refuse others the right to have a sex and make use of it as they please. . . . The Bourgeoisie's 'blood' was its sex."[20] Likewise, in *Discipline and Punish* Foucault maps the supersession of the modern juridical subject over the "real" body and blood of the medieval condemned.[21]

In spite of his desire to "transform history into a totally different form of time," traditional history most haunted Foucault in his schemes of periodization, the normativity of which has come under the scrutiny of critics such as Michel de Certeau, Homi Bhabha, and

Eve Kosofsky Sedgwick.[22] As early as 1974 de Certeau worried about the "ethnological" *form* (his emphasis) of Foucault's genealogy.[23] By ethnological form he meant Foucault's paradoxical strengthening of Enlightenment notions of progress in his "cutting out" and "turning-over" its illegitimate discourses in order to have them serve as a resource for an ethnographic writing of alien bodies (the "mad," the "prisoner," the "homosexual"). Foucault's genealogical practice inverted the high points of the Enlightenment chronology of progress to one of temporal breaks. Bhabha has shown how Foucault's genealogy collaborates with traditional history, since it fabricates the space in which to locate the "that was then" of medieval regimes of blood.[24] Sedgwick has cautioned that genealogical history has not only reified the conventional premodern/modern divide; it has also reified the "now" as a knowable, coherent temporal field.[25] The temporal *form* of traditional periodization ("that was then, this is now") thus colonizes the *content* of Foucault's discursive analyses. The colonizing medium is sanguinity, an important substance in the Christian typological imaginary.

Sanguinity

Foucault argued that "blood was a reality with a symbolic function" and that this premodern reality was eclipsed by a modern society of sex.[26] Sex did not work as a symbol but rather as an object or target: "the new procedures of power that were devised during the classical age and employed in the nineteenth century were what caused our societies to go from a *symbolics of blood* to an *analytics of sexuality*."[27]

Foucault used blood as an ethnographic substance to mark the "that was then" of the European premodern and he read sexuality as the sign of the modern—"this is now." He condensed this temporal binary in the bourgeois body: "the bourgeoisie's 'blood' was its sex." In her rereading of Foucault, Ann Laura Stoler reminds us that if modern sex affirmed the bourgeois's body in the European metropolis, blood with its leakage negated such unitary fantasy in the colonies.[28] Along the intimate fold of metropolis and colony a discourse of blood *doubles* a genealogy of sexuality. Put more broadly, the intimate fold between sexuality and blood marks what Homi Bhabha has called the resemblance and menace of colonial mimicry: "it is as if the very emergence of the 'colonial' is dependent for its representation upon some strategic limitation or prohibition within the authoritative discourse itself."[29]

Foucault's genealogy, rooted as it is in a notion of supersession, could not think the juridical subject that might reside within premodern regimes of blood. His model of supersession thus repeats the double graphic of blood already noted in the discussion of the engraving of Simon of Trent. Foucauldian genealogy cannot interrogate this double graphic in order to "disinscribe" it. Contemporary historians of medieval history inform us that blood is not some "natural" substance, but rather a legal fluid fabricated in the courts of medieval Europe to mark first the difference within (such as Irish and Anglo-Irish) and the difference between a newly emerging biological theology of Christian and Jewish difference. Such fabrication of blood became constititutive of new regimes of "nature" (and not vice versa). Laws against miscegenation prescribed sanguinary borders both between Christians (intra-sanguinary borders) and between Christian and Jew (inter-sanguinary borders).[30] His genealogical method, indeed, his archaeology of knowledge, constitutes an ongoing work in the typological imaginary: "what we try to examine is the incision that it makes, that irreducible—and very often tiny—emergence."[31] The incision of Foucauldian genealogy remains paradoxically encrypted in the register of incisions recorded so far in this study of the Christian typological imaginary.

What Foucault mostly refuses to address in his genealogical study of texts, archives, artifacts, is the question of traumatic repetition, and the relation of repetition to his notions of rupture and discontinuity.[32] I have joined discussion of Foucault with Altdorfer and the inquisition, a collage that might at first have seemed capricious to some readers, to show the *consequences* of repetition in the Christian typological imaginary. This chapter has argued that we can only begin to intervene in repetitions of the Christian typological imaginary by recognizing them. The eunuchs of history despised by Foucault offer us a cautionary lesson about the "knowledge made for cutting" that genealogy is.[33] No cut is ever a clean one, as repetition of the Christian typological imaginary tragically teaches.

Chapter 4
Lachrymose History, the Typological Imaginary, and the Lacanian Enlightenment

[For this reason,] there were but a few written laws; and even those were not completely intelligible without oral instruction and tradition. Nevertheless, it was forbidden to add explanations and comments in writing. It was the unwritten laws, the oral tradition, and the living instruction from person to person and from *mouth to mouth* that were to explain, enlarge, limit, or define more clearly what, by wise intent and wise moderation, had been left undefined in the written law.

—Mendelssohn, *Jerusalem*

Mouth to Mouth

In 1783, when Moses Mendelssohn (1729–86) published his treatise entitled *Jerusalem*, he wrote at length of the graphic deadness of the Christian dead letter ("everything is reduced to the dead letter").[1] This morbidity provoked him to meditate on the origins of writing and the relationship of deafness to writing. He based his defense of Judaism as revealed law (in contradistinction to revealed religion) on an intriguing acoustical argument about the distinctive properties of Jewish dialogue. He wrote that Jewish truths "could not have been inspired through direct revelation: indeed, they could not have been made known through *speech* or *writing*, which can be understood only here and now."[2] By positing something in between speech and writing, Mendelssohn, I contend, broached the concept "unhistorical." He imagined Jewish dialogue as the excess of both speech and writing (as vital as mouth to mouth resuscitation). His work can provide an unhistorical model for rethinking the Christian typological imaginary. This chapter explores Mendelssohn's vision as a way of providing an unhistorical history of acoustics in the Christian typological imaginary. Rather than posit a "that was then" cut away from a "this is now" to distinguish Christians from Jews, Mendelssohn, instead, concentrated on the space in between the letter and spirit and listened to the echoes that resonated in that gap.

Mendelssohn's *Jerusalem* takes this chapter into the "homeland of allegory" (Walter Benjamin's term) to explore how an echo might resonate in Jewish-Christian dialogue.[3] I take Mendelssohn's concerns with deafness (a shared interest among Enlightenment philosophers) as my starting point for thinking about the contemporary historiographical debate over lachrymose history, or Jammergeschichte. These are terms first coined by Salo Wittmayer Baron (1895–1989) in the 1920s. Now in a new century, a new generation of medieval scholars such as David Nirenberg and Miri Rubin question the tradition of lachryomose history in their writing on medieval Christian-Jewish relations.[4] Mendelssohn's work cautioned me to listen for an acoustical crisis in the modern vicissitudes of lachrymose history. I wanted to understand how Mendelssohn's acoustical argument about Jewish dialogue gets trivialized and muffled as "jammer."

Baron, the first scholar to hold an endowed chair in Jewish history at a secular university, epitomized his critique of lachrymose history in 1928 in the American journal *Menorah*. Born in Tarnov (Galicia) and a graduate of the University of Vienna, where he earned three doctorates, Baron had joined the faculty of the Jewish Institute of Religion in New York in 1926. In 1929, he was chosen to fill the Miller Professorship of "Jewish history, literature, and institutions" at Columbia University. His 1928 essay, "Ghetto and Emancipation," traced Jammergeschichte to a medieval Ashkenazi tradition, which, he claimed, emplotted Jewish history since the fall of the temple as a lamentable vale of tears. Baron further argued that some Jewish historians of the nineteenth century remobilized the tradition to aid civic assimilation. Baron intended that his oeuvre, a legacy of social and economic studies of European Jews, should mute such lachrymosity once and for all. However, to his chagrin, he claimed that scholars at the Hebrew University in Jerusalem, which opened its doors in 1925, were extending the tradition.

In the *Menorah* article Baron laid the chief blame for the institutionalization of lachrymose history at the door of Wissenschaft des Judentums, an intellectual movement that advocated the study of Jewish texts according to the criteria of modern, scientific scholarship and placed the investigation of the Jewish past in a firm historical mold. In 1819 a group of Jewish scholars and rabbis, notably Eduard

Gans (1796–1839), Leopold Zunz (1794–1886), Isaac Marcus Jost (1793–1860), Moses Moser (1796–1838), and Isaac Levin Auerbach (1791–1853), came together in Berlin to form the Verein für Kulturwissenschaft des Judentums. Baron ascribed to this group a political project of rendering Jewish emancipation palatable to the modern German state. In order to disarm the notion that Jews constituted a "state within a state," scholars of the Wissenschaft argued that Jews as a political entity ceased to exist after the destruction of the second temple.[5] Thus exile (*galut*) marked almost two millennia of nonsovereignty. According to Baron, it was in the best interests of these nineteenth-century historians to argue for the utility of political emancipation by exaggerating the "Dark Ages" of Judaism.[6] Baron regarded their agenda as intrinsic to their overlapping activities of liturgical reform and also, paradoxically, compatible with an organized Zionist agenda emergent in the latter part of the nineteenth century.

Baron concluded his essay with a strong programmatic statement:

Certainly its belief in the efficacy of a process of complete assimilation has been proved untenable. Autonomy as well as equality must be given its place in the modern State, and much time must pass before these two principles will be fully harmonized and balanced. Perhaps the chief task of this and future generations is to attain that harmony and balance. Surely it is time to break with the lachrymose theory of pre-Revolutionary woe, and to adopt a view more in accord with historic truth.[7]

Recent scholarship has questioned Baron's harsh rebuke of Wissenschaft des Judentums. The inauguration of modern Jewish studies in nineteenth-century Germany, scholars now contend, did not align itself on a simple, linear model of assimilation. For instance, Susannah Heschel reads the work of Abraham Geiger (1810–74), a noted Orientalist and Reform rabbi who attempted to write a history of Christianity from a Jewish perspective, as one of the earliest examples of postcolonial writings among Jewish intellectuals.[8] David Sorkin also refigures the intellectual and political activity of Wissenschaft des Judentums by exploring its complex antecedents in the early Enlightenment. He observes how emergent schools of utilitarianism, which posed the question of how Jews could be made useful to the state, politicized the Enlightenment agenda.

Such studies as these by Heschel and Sorkin caution against dichotomizing lachrymose history and the so-called "rational" approaches to Jewish history advocated by Baron. Yet just such binaries still persist in the debate over lachrymose history. Take, for example, the two recent studies already discussed in the introduction to this book?—David Nirenberg's *Communities of Violence* and Miri Rubin's

Gentile Tales. They map the boundary between lachrymosity and rationality as a divide between psychoanalysis and history. Nirenberg
lumps together studies as methodologically diverse as Norman Cohn's
Europe's Inner Demons (1975), Robert Moore's *The Foundation of a Persecuting Society* (1987), and Carlo Ginzburg's *Ecstasies* (1991) as exercises in "psychoanalysis."[9] He pits the rational study of historical
analysis against "psychoanalysis" and in so doing inadvertently forecloses the historical study of dynamic and changing social imaginaries.
So constrained, the binary between lachrymosity and rationality in
Nirenberg's book perforce lapses into functionalism grounded in the
individual choices of historical actors. Nirenberg has to make the
"utilitarian" argument (an argument that haunted Enlightenment discourse only to return unanalyzed here) that violence is usable. By
insisting on a binary he cannot ask broader, historiographical questions about the historical emergence of utilitarianism and its repetition in his own study on Christian-Jewish relations.

In *Gentile Tales*, Miri Rubin, like Nirenberg, also relies on a belief in
transcendent freedom in order to make a claim for individual choices
to resist the violence encoded in the host desecration narratives she
studies. Yet both authors have difficulty demonstrating specific
instances of such individual resistance. This impasse around choice
convinces me that historians need a history of lachrymose history.
Is there something about lamentation itself, trapped as it is in the
word Jammergeschichte (Baron's polemical and deeply abjecting term),
to which historians need to attend? *Gentile Tales* offers an important
clue to lamentation as an unvoiced problem in the study of medieval
Christian-Jewish relations. In an appendix to this work Rubin offers
her own translation of the liturgical poem "All the afflictions which
have befallen us" ("Et kol ha-tela'a") by Rabbi Avigdor Kara of Prague
(d. 1439).[10] This "heart-rending lament" was recited during the after-
noon prayers of the Day of Atonement according to the liturgical use
of Prague. Her folding of this medieval lament within a more general
critique of lachrymose history deeply interested me. It inspired me to
ask about the vicissitudes of Ashkenazi lamentation in the Reform
movement inspired by Wissenschaft des Judentums.[11]

My study (limited to mostly German publications since I do not
read Hebrew) followed the story of the muting of Ashkenazi lamentation in new synagogue liturgies devised in the wake of the Jewish
Enlightenment. The great nineteenth-century Jewish theologian Abraham Geiger shaped the story I have pieced together. Upon receiving
his doctorate from the University of Marburg and his reception as a
rabbi in 1834, Geiger went to serve the Wiesbaden synagogue. As one
of his first reforming steps, he abolished the recitation of medieval

Hebrew poems of lamentation during the traditional period of mourning for the destruction of the second temple. The reaction against these poems involved more than questions of their content. Linguistic reason was at stake. A move toward sundering Ashkenazi lamentation from the liturgy had already been voiced as early as 1786, when David Friedländer, a key figure of the Jewish Enlightenment, urged, in his German translation of the Ashkenazi prayer book, that prayer be linked to "reason." Later, in 1812, he directly criticized "the prayers and melodies that had become increasingly strange to both father and child, increasingly dispensable, increasingly out of harmony with the newly acquired concepts."[12] What "tinkled" (his words), what bore no "echo" of religious consciousness, had to go. An early Reform ordinance instituted in 1810 in a Westphalian synagogue exemplified this new attention to the "modernity" of the voice in the synagogue liturgy: "Every cantor shall endeavor to enunciate every word of the prayers clearly. The unsuitable traditional singing which interrupts the prayers is to be avoided. Every accompaniment by singers and bass-singers, employed by some congregations for that purpose, is to cease altogether."[13] Rabbinical guidelines drawn up in 1845 for liturgical performance of holy day services in Berlin register a radical limit of liturgical reform. Reform rabbis agreed that German was to be used throughout the entire service with a few exceptions; that the shofar would not be blown; that the head would be uncovered for worship; that there would intermission addresses (vernacular preaching) on the Day of Atonement; that use of the tallith would be discontinued; that women would sing in the choir; and that men and women would be seated on the same floor.[14]

At the same time as they implemented liturgical reform, rabbis also fiercely debated the binding status of ritual and dietary laws, circumcision, the authority of the Talmud, and the revision of a version of Messianic theology grounded in a return to Palestine as a homeland.[15] Such liturgical and theological debate was intertwined with the editing projects underway among the scholars of Wissenschaft des Judentums. One of these great undertakings, the pathbreaking history of vernacular synagogue preaching (1842) and subsequent publications on medieval synagogue poetry by Leopold Zunz, seem, at first glance, to be magnificent examples of scholarly recuperation. Yet a closer look reveals deep ambivalence, especially on the subject of medieval Ashkenazi poetry. It is telling to read how Zunz describes the kind of poetry written by medieval rabbis such as Rabbi Avigdor Kara as "difficult, dark, untranslatable."[16] A contemporary of Zunz and fellow scholar of medieval Hebrew literature, Moritz Steinschneider (1816–1907), polemically articulated such ambivalence by declaring that their work was to bury the remnants of Judaism."[17] In his important reference work, *Hebräische Übersetzungen* (1858–65), Steinschneider actually excluded many translations of medieval German Jewish literature. He thought that the Ashkenazi material (in contrast to highly valued Sephardic poetry) offered only "sad themes."[18] In sum, liturgical reform and scholarly publications of the mid-nineteenth century had the effect of encrypting medieval Ashkenazi lamentation. Over the crypt, reformists built temple organs, and trained choirs in German hymnody; in other words, they substituted a decorous, domesticated acoustics for what they considered to be the lamentation of the "Dark Ages."

Through such selective procedures in scholarly publication and liturgical performance, reformers and Wissenschaft scholars pitted reason and intelligibility against the vicissitudes and strangeness of the voice. They sought to exclude what they came to regard as a "Dark Age" voice—a voice that sticks in the throat of history. Baron's abjecting critique of lachrymose history, its designation as Jammergeschichte, emerged from this cultural milieu. Reason comes to rule the voice at the expense of lamentation. Indeed, it is as if reforming rabbis imagined acoustical reason "superseding" irrational Ashkenazi lamentation.

Lamentation and Psychoanalysis

The question of Wissenschaft des Judentums and lachrymose history becomes even more complicated when it is approached from the perspective of psychoanalysis and the emergence of the psychoanalytic subject.[19] Scholars of psychoanalysis usually date the appearance of the psychoanalytic subject to the Enlightenment, but to a Kantian Enlightenment unencumbered by the Jewish Haskalah. Some recent work, however, suggests the impossibility of separating the Haskalah from Aufklärung.[20] For the purposes of my argument, I want to show what is at stake in ignoring the Haskalah in this psychoanalytic scheme of periodization. But first some more detail on the psychoanalytic arguments for linking the psychoanalytic subject with the Kantian Enlightenment. Lacanian analysts, in particular, emphatically mark the Kantian Enlightenment as the origin of the psychoanalytic subject. Scholars such as Copjec, Žižek, and Dolar use a theological argument to divide premodernity from modernity. According to them there can be no pre-Enlightenment psychoanalytic subject, because, they argue, in premodern times theology and the holy mapped onto each other. The theological and the sacred were coincident. It is only when Enlightenment philosophers, Kant being exemplary, broke up the theological subject that the conditions of modernity could emerge and with it the psychoanalytic subject. They designate the sign of fracture in theological space, or the ambit of the sacred, as the *uncanny*. They define the uncanny as the alien (theological) kernel lodged within the modern (secular) subject. Mladen Dolar goes further and contradicts Freud, who had claimed that the uncanny was the return of something long ago surmounted. For Dolar the uncanny emerged with and is constitutive of both the Enlightenment and psychoanalysis. The uncanny, for Lacanians, is about "this is now." By implication, the uncanny can only be thought of as marking secular supersession over the theological. The holy, "contained" theologically as Dolar claims it was in the premodern, is superseded by the modern uncanny, which lurks in the heart of the secularized, transcendental subject.

Herein lies the crux of psychoanalytic periodization. By insisting that the uncanny marks the divide between "the psychoanalytic now" and "the premodern then," Lacanians make it impossible to think of the uncanny simultaneously as both historical and unhistorical, secular and sacred (indeed, sacred in different forms: Jewish, Christian, Muslim). Psychoanalytic models of periodization paradoxically enact another profound disciplinary anxiety as well. In their exclusive concentration on Kant, psychoanalytic theorists, like most Enlightenment scholars, cannot imagine reading Kant side by side with Mendelssohn, his brilliant philosophical double and an observant Jew. In spite of his profound challenge to Kant's conception of religion, Mendelssohn, a major Enlightenment thinker and leader of the Haskalah, is almost always relegated to the historiographical margins of Enlightenment studies. Were eighteenth-century scholars to try to reposition Mendelssohn, they would inevitably come up against Kant's move to reoccupy the grounds of scriptural hermeneutics. By this I mean that Kant attempted to rationalize Christian typology, the millennium-old figural practice of reading the letter for the spirit. Any attempt to read Kant and Mendelssohn together would have to be wary of falling into the typological trap set up by Kant: which thinker, then, would prefigure whom, that is, who should be read as the letter and who be read as the spirit? The Lacanian "uncanny" marks this supersession of the secular over the theological. However, such models of supersession, viewed from the perspective of the Haskalah, look more complex, less binary. Something in between the letter and the spirit reverberates at the crossroads of their proposed supersession. When they are considered together the Enlightenment uncanny acquires an echo. This echo, I argue, can be heard in Freud's 1919 essay on the uncanny, even though Lacanians have ignored it.[21]

Freud and Echo

All that is to live in endless song
Must in life-time first be drown'd
(Freud, citing Schiller)[22]

Before turning to Freud's essay on the uncanny, I want to consider one of his earlier discussions published in the *The Interpretation of Dreams* (1899). In his report of a childhood nightmare, he exemplifies his acoustical methodologies of interpretation. The way in which he sounded out his dream provides crucial evidence for considering his arguments about the uncanny. He narrated his early dream thus:

It was very vivid and showed me my beloved mother with a distinctively tranquil, sleeping, expression on her face, who was being carried into the room by two (or three) persons with birds' beaks, and laid on the bed.[23]

Consistent with interpreting the dream as a narrative of oedipal desire and religious taboo, Freud related the word "Vogel" (bird) to the German slang for intercourse ("vögeln") and to the image of the bird-headed Egyptian deities that he saw pictured in the family Bible, which so fascinated him in childhood.[24] His acoustical method of sounding out the dream enabled him to fabricate a sound track for the silent dream image. First he voiced *Vogel* and then echoed the word with an added "n." True to his method, Freud substitutes words for images: "The words which are put together in this way are no longer nonsensical but may form a poetical phrase of the greatest beauty and significance."[25] For the sake of producing his oedipal interpretation, Freud had to mute other parts of his dream. What is at stake, I wondered, in these unsounded parts?

The psychoanalytic concept of the "object" voice helped me to explore the sound track that Freud fabricated so masterfully for his dream. Mladen Dolar has defined the "object" voice as a kind of acoustical antithesis of the mother's voice, which for the infant resounds with choric plenitude. In contrast to the mother's voice, the "object" voice paradoxically sounds the dissolution of the voice in all its imagined positivity of self-presence and auto-affection.[26] The object voice questions the narcissistic fantasy of mastery over one's own voice. What strikes most about Freud's sound track is his insistence on sounding out his childhood dream in German. At his natal home in Príbor (Freiburg, Moravia) at least four languages (Yiddish, German, Czech, Polish) surrounded Freud. His mother, remembered by her grandson as a "typical Polish Jewess," most likely spoke to her son in

Yiddish. His Catholic nanny, who cared for him until he was two and one-half years old, presumably spoke Czech and German. His father, Jakob Freud, spoke Hebrew as well as German or better, as Freud later recalled.[27]

The monophonic German sound track of his dream analysis silences this linguistic polyphony of his childhood. He also leaves unsounded the powerful dream image of his mother. What if Freud had voiced a sound for the image of his mother, say, something acoustically "nonsensical" like "Mama" or, keeping in mind those bird-like figures, "Vogelsänger," that is "warbler"? Since the image of the mother is deathlike (reminding him, he wrote, of the face of his comatose grandfather just before his death), would "mama," "warbler," sound more than nonsensical, perhaps lamentable? Is it possible to imagine the German in his sound track as a kind of acoustical *disguise* for the disturbing object voice, the disintegrated maternal voice, that Freud avoids?

The question of acoustical disguise comes to the fore in Freud's essay on the uncanny. Most significantly therein, Freud rules out the voice as a source of the uncanny. The uncanny for him is an optical phenomenon. His exclusion of the voice is most marked in the lengthy section of the essay in which he offers a reading of "The Sandman," a well-known short story by E. T. A. Hoffmann. First, Freud dismisses the opinion of commentators who regarded the automaton, Olympia, with its (her) mechanized speech (limited to the exclamation, "ach") as the uncanny character in the story. Instead, Freud focuses on specularity as source of the uncanny in this story. According to Freud, the fear of losing one's eyes, of having them picked out by the owl-like children of the Sandman as punishment for naughtiness, is the source of the uncanny because such an image arouses the child's fear of castration.[28] Fear, for Freud, is induced optically, not acoustically. Freud further genitalizes the uncanny by relating the German word for the uncanny ("unheimlich") to the womb ("heim").[29] By so doing he anxiously forecloses the consideration of other corporeal cavities and their possible relations to the uncanny.

Freud's insistence on the uncanny as a visual phenomenon in his reading of Hoffmann effectively silences a very noisy story filled with a babble of voices that stick in the throat. To offer just a few examples: it is the nursery voice of the nanny that first terrifies the protagonist Nathaniel. This old woman tells the story of the Sandman whose children look not unlike the bird-creatures in Freud's dream of his mother. The voice of the dark character with a dual identity, Coppelius-Coppola, also reverberates in the text. It is described by Hoffmann as "muffled and menacing" (dumpfer, drohender) (21);

"hissing and lisping" (zischte und lispelte) (23); "grating" (räuspern) (95). Coppelius-Coppola speaks in a kind of nonsense pidgin. Confused by the optical conundrum of this doppelgänger, Nathaniel tries to persuade himself that Coppelius is not Coppola on the basis of accent: "one can tell from his accent that he is really a Piedmontese. Coppelius was a German" ("und überdem hört man es auch seiner Aussprache an, daß er wirklich Piemonteser ist. Coppelius war ein Deutscher" [48]).[30] Nathaniel not only sees things, as Freud reminds us, but he hears things as well, as Freud neglects to notice. For instance, as he writes a poem for the heroine he is carried away by a fantasy that overpowers him acoustically (76). Only the voice of Clara is able to break through his auditory hallucination.

The oral cavity, I argue, haunts Hoffmann's story, and I want to argue that it haunts Freud's essay on the uncanny. The tale stages the contradictory relations of the voice to language in key ways. Hoffmann poses the problem of voice specifically as a question of seeing with your ears. He writes about acoustical transmission as a slow, laborious process subject to vicissitudes. He foregrounds this acoustical process by creating a female pair of doppelgänger—Clara the betrothed of Nathaniel, and Olympia the automaton. The author's demonstration of seeing with your ears occurs in a crucial passage, in which he has poets, who are gazing on a painted image of Clara, address the reader:

That is nonsense about a lake and a mirror. Can we look at the girl without sensing heavenly music, which flows into us from her glance and penetrates to the very soul until everything within us stirs awake and pulsates with emotion? And, if we cannot then sing splendid tunes, we are not worth much; the smile flitting about her lips will tell us this clearly enough when we have the courage to squeak out in her presence something which we profess to be a song when, in fact, it is only a disconnected jumble of notes strung together.[31]

Hoffmann's poetic characters, gazing on an image, hear what they see. Clara's image broadcasts song and music. Yet, something goes awry with the reception. The poets, according to their confession, are not able to reproduce this sound with any fidelity. What comes out are squeaks and confused notes; they sound like children who are just learning how to talk, or better how to read. Hoffmann, in fact, is depicting a scene that resonates (uncannily) with important historical changes in pedagogical practices of his day. In his study of discourse networks at the turn of 1800, Friedrich Kittler has shown how European alphabets underwent oralization in early childhood pedagogy of the time.[32] Pedagogues transformed the traditional method of learning by graphic rote, whereby a child associated a written letter with a sound and then spelled out the word letter by letter. In the new and widely disseminated *syllabic* method, relegated to the mother as her responsibility, the mother sounded out words, syllable by syllable, and her children attended to the shaping of her lips and the sound of voice, and not to written letters, to learn their alphabet. It is the mother who now teaches reading orally by turning words into a string of syllables not unlike musical notes. The new phonetic method produced a body that "has eyes and ears only in order to be a large mouth."[33] Kittler further describes how good mothers engaged in their own self-education to produce such acoustical effects: "Self-education dismissed imitative learning and produced pure pronunciation for its motherly teachers through a methodical exploration of the oral cavity."[34]

Hoffmann's description of the poets viewing Clara's image intuits the uncanny acoustical nature of this powerful reform pedagogy underway in Germany. Its new practices put the mother into the position of Echo. She does not speak a word. In the intentional moment of pedagogy, the mother's voice echoes as pure form, contentless, a syllabic vector unfilled with the subject's intention, in other words, the object voice.[35] The child, therefore, experiences the mother's voice metamorphosed into the object voice in the nursery schoolroom. In such lessons, the two voices, the maternal voice as acoustical mirror and the object voice as instrument and initiator of a national pedagogy, are both uncannily separated and contiguous in the nursery. To keep the object voice of pedagogy, which haunts the maternal voice, safely noncontiguous, one can mechanize the voice. But such technological intervention only compounds the uncanny. Hence, the acoustical implications of reform pedagogy offer a context for understanding the anxious dissemination of talking automata (materially and fictionally) in late eighteenth-century Europe. Given Hoffmann's staging of the object voice lurking within the mother's teaching voice, as expressed in the direct address of the poets to Clara's image, it is not surprising, indeed it is almost predictable, that he should have to write a talking automaton in his text. He constructs Clara and Olympia as acoustical doppelgänger. Olympia's uncanny mechanized voice can keep at bay the perceived feminization and infantilization of the poet's speech when these poets hear what they see.

But this neat and highly gendered pedagogical division of labor resonating around the mother's mouth and the child's eyes and ears grows more complicated when we turn away from Kittler's national narrative to consider Freud's own education. Freud's father, according to family reports, tutored him at home until he was nine years old. He then went on to enroll in the Leopoldstädter Kommunal

Real-und Obergymnasium in Vienna where he became an immediate success.[36] Let us imagine the scene of pedagogy at home among the Freuds. Jakob Freud is sounding out the syllables of German to his son, who watches his father's mouth and lips in order to learn the sounds. Did he do the same when his father intoned the music of Hebrew accents that transformed consonants into syllables?[37] Did he fall in love with the "mouth instrument" of his father, as Kittler claims that most proper German children would have fallen in love with their mother's mouth, who, as the usually designated teacher of the young, bore the avowed responsibility of training children for the state?[38] Educational primers and tracts, written for mothers at the time that Jakob Freud tutored his son, scientifically diagrammed the passageways, orifices, and depths of the mother's mouth and throat, the very folds that were eroticized for the child in the reading lesson. The familiar oedipal chain used by contemporary scholars to "analyze" Freud retrospectively, linked as it is around his circumcision, misses, I contend, the father's mouth as a vital and queer area of his early eroticization. The father's mouth and throat, in the pedagogical case of Sigmund Freud, exposed him to a sense of interiority as he learned, and the sounds that emanated from the father's throat would break down simple fictions of the body as an enclosed package. Jakob Freud and Echo would seem to be closely bound if we read them through childhood pedagogy.

Freud, however, carefully choked off the mouth and throat in his analysis of the "Sandman."[39] He buried the talking automaton, Olympia, in a footnote where he discussed Nathaniel's narcissism and identified the automaton as the "personification of Nathaniel's feminine attitude towards his father in his infancy."[40] Since Freud anxiously buried Olympia and her echolalia in a footnote to his essay on the uncanny, and since he studiously avoided discussion of Echo in his myriad publications about Narcissus, perhaps it is necessary to consider further Jakob Freud and his son in an effort to understand the relations of echo to the uncanny in Freud's work.

Freud and Circumcision

"I have put upon it a cover of new skin and have called it: "Spring up, O well, sing ye unto it." (translation of Jakob Freud's Hebrew inscription to his son, 1891)[41]

In 1891, on the occasion of his son's thirty-fifth birthday, Jakob Freud presented him with the family Bible. He inscribed it with a moving Hebrew poem, a verse of which serves as the epigram for this section. The father writes that he wishes his son to sing. Jakob Freud also rebound the Bible in a new skin, one that he imagined as a singing skin. Once again, acoustics come to the fore with the father and son. The question of these singing skins takes us from Freud's essay on the uncanny to his discussion of circumcision in *Moses and Monotheism.* In his last completed book, Freud comes closest to Mendelssohn and his theory of the acoustic in Jewish dialogue. Echo, whom he had so rigorously excluded in his analytical writings on narcissism, resounds in *Moses and Monotheism.* In this much debated work Freud provides us with an acoustical medium for reading the echoes of the uncanny in his oeuvre.

In *Moses and Monotheism* Freud ambitiously attempted to join history, linguistic theory, psychoanalysis. He uses circumcision to join his history of the vicissitudes of Jewish tradition and his theory of sexuality. He frequently refers to circumcision as uncanny (*unheimlich*).[42] According to Freud, the cut of the foreskin reminds men of the first sexual cut, the killing of the father by the horde of brothers:

Circumcision is the symbolical substitute of castration, a punishment which the primeval father dealt his sons long ago and out of the fullness of his power; and whosoever accepted this symbol showed by so doing that he was ready to submit to the father's will, although it was at the cost of a painful sacrifice.[43]

Recently critics have begun to devote more attention to Freud's privileging of circumcision in this text. Historicist readings of race and gender in nineteenth-century eugenics have shown how this discourse imagined circumcision as castrating and feminizing. Such abjection, they argue, caused Freud to produce his theory of castration as a traumatic substitution for the rite of circumcision. In keeping with the specular language of the sign (*Zeichen, Abzeichen*) used by Freud in *Moses and Monotheism* to describe circumcision, critics have tended to emphasize the gaze and circumcision.[44] They do so, I argue, at the expense of analyzing crucial links he makes between voice, language, and circumcision in that essay. He uses these acoustical concerns to knot together his theories of Jewish history, traumatic wounding, and sexuality.

Freud's concept of "tradition" in *Moses and Monotheism* becomes the site for his acoustical theorizing. According to Freud, it was tradition, as disseminated through the songs of the Prophets, that remembered the repressed history of Moses (his injunction of circumcision) and his death. They "preached" ("verkündeten") the "old Mosaic doctrine;" they "gave [it] their voice" ("ihre Stimme liehen").[45] The "voice of the Prophets" ("die Stimme der Propheten") remembers traumatic events that written texts would forget: "What is deleted or altered in the written version might quite well have been preserved uninjured in the tradition."[46] Freud then sets up a compelling parallel between his historical argument for oral tradition and his psychoanalytical theory of trauma. He links trauma with early childhood and pinpoints such trauma to the time when the child is learning to speak: "Impressions during the time when the child begins to speak are found to be especially interesting."[47] Freud then proceeds anxiously to erase the importance of his proposal about acoustical traumata (things heard), which he just asserted, by introducing the specular image of "screen memories" ("Deckerinerungen").[48] He uses an analogy to the chemistry of photographic development to illustrate the temporal ways in which latency surfaces in trauma. But he does not manage to repress his acoustical theory of trauma completely. He retrieves his arguments about hearing, speech, and language in a subsequent and much commented upon section, when he tries to describe the transmission of historical trauma over time to human populations. He sees such transmission occurring via a phylogenetic concept of speech acquisition: "Here there seems to be an assured case of archaic inheritance from the time when speech was developing."[49]

Freud goes back and forth between his acoustical and specular accounts of trauma in *Moses and Monotheism*. He also sets up other complementary parallelisms: two people, two kingdoms, two names, two new religions, two founders of a religion, two narratives (oral and written). Only one trace of trauma in his account cuts across his dualistic reconstruction of Jewish religious history: and that is circumcision, which he dubbed a "leitfossil."[50] Out of the wound of the excised foreskin Freud told the suppressed history of Moses the Egyptian. He conceived of circumcision as like a gramophone—the wound is the one recording device that records and retains sense and nonsense without discrimination. In an interesting qualification to his argument, Freud made it clear that a tradition based only on oral tradition, without repression, could not produce the religious phenomena in which he was interested. Circumcision performs such repression and memorializes it. Therefore, the prophets insisted on this rite in their oral tradition. Circumcision is compellingly uncanny in *Moses and Monotheism*, not because it substitutes for castration, as Freud insisted, but because it is an acoustical record for the prophet's mouth. The Hebrew word for making a covenant, "karat berit," includes the word *to cut*. Freud's argument for circumcision in *Moses and Monotheism* works like an acoustical cut to the prophet's mouth. In his last publication, Freud produced what his father wished for him— a singing skin. The uncanny father's mouth becomes the echo of the foreskin in Freud's story about the importance of a repressed oral tradition marked by circumcision.

Echo Returns

Freud, as I have already noted, consistently avoided Echo in his various discussions of Narcissus and narcissism. He avoided, too, most discussion of the voice as a narcissistic object. His study *Moses and Monotheism*, in which he posits the "unheimlich" of castration as precisely its acoustical properties of marking the "alien" prophetic kernel within oral tradition, helps us to understand the acoustics he so anxiously elided in his earlier essay on the uncanny. My own reading of that essay has attempted to uncrypt Echo in order to open up the space in between castration and circumcision in Freud's work and to tell a tale of a disavowed erotics of the father's mouth. It is Echo, too, who now needs also to intervene among the contemporary historicists who eschew lachrymose history without acknowledging the historiographical problem of thinking Enlightenment and Haskalah together —Kant with Mendelssohn. Mendelssohn's understanding of Jewish dialogue asks us to think of Echo as an unhistorical acoustic between speech and writing between the circumcision of the foreskin and of the heart. There is much to be learned from his plea for the unhistorical. It recasts the timing of the typological imaginary, the psychoanalytical subject, of "Western" modernity. Supersession repeats itself in modernity as none other than the "crafting of myths of modernity precisely out of the religious material that formed such an important part of [their] early modern day vocabularies."[51]

Chapter 5
Translating the Foreskin

Cutting Up History

This chapter explores the fantasy of the clean cut that supersession is by using eunuchs as a way of thinking about cutting. In so doing, it does not attempt to be either a chronological study or a social history of eunuchs, although John Boswell wrote in 1991 that such a history was "badly needed."[1] Rather, I come to focus on how eunuchs often appear as a kind of "period piece" at sites of conflict between supersession and the unhistorical.[2] I have already shown how Foucault, in his essay "Nietzsche, Genealogy, History," used the eunuch as a trope to denigrate the "traditional historian."[3] His famous genealogical maxim, "knowledge made for cutting," severs the eunuch from the epistemological desires of genealogy. It is as if the eunuch works as a kind of fetish image for Foucault; that is, the eunuch flashes as the last image of traditional history that genealogy sees before its methodological break. In so fetishizing the eunuch, Foucault, as Chapter 3 proposed, had foreclosed a study of the unhistorical. This chapter seeks to open up a gap in the fetish of supersession. It explores interstices—between the testicles and the penis, between "that was then, this was now."

It begins with a reading of Freud's essay on fetishism where the circumcised foreskin is at stake and then turns to the trouble with circumcision that emerges in the historico-ethnographic study of Amitav Ghosh entitled *In an Antique Land*.[4] The chapter uses Freud and Ghosh as a way of thinking discursively about the intersections between the fetishized corporeal organization of archivist, fieldworker, and historian and the rigid temporality of supersession ("that was then, this is now").

The Fetish of Supersession

In 1927, Freud published his essay on fetishism. It opens with a Freudian slip that offers a vantage point onto the construction of historical Jewish difference. I want to show first how Freud's slip helps us to translate the fetish from individual psychology to institutional politics. Then I want to pass through this Freudian loophole to the Mediterranean trading diaspora of the twelfth century described by Amitav Ghosh in his book, *In an Antique Land*. At stake in my return to Freud's fetishism is an effort to understand the repetition of historical trauma at work in supersession. In such belatedness historians can construct a much-needed ethical relation to the political project of rethinking supersession.

The essay on fetishism opens with an exercise in translation. Freud begins by discussing the renowned fetish of his analysand the Wolf Man, who had a particular concern with a "shine on the nose" ("Glanz auf der Nase"). As Freud says, "he exalted a certain sort of 'shine on the nose' into a fetishistic precondition."[5] Because Freud knew that the Wolf Man heard English spoken in his nursery by his childhood nurse, he translated the German homonymically into English. The German "Glanz auf der Nase" thus becomes the English "glance at the nose."[6] Freud breaks off this story here, never to take it up again in the essay.

This clean break warrants attention. *Glanz* and *glance* also echo the obvious, nearly homonymic, medical term, *glans*, the anatomical word for the head of the penis *or* the clitoris. Nevertheless, Freud, the physician, does not sound out this alternative for the reader. His silence raises questions about the circulation of Freud's own trauma in his essay on fetishism. What exactly is Freud modeling in his opening anecdote? According to Freud, the fetish encoded (in his words) the "last impression received before the uncanny traumatic one."[7] Could it be that the *Glanz, glance* of the Wolf Man covers over the corporeal trauma of the *glans* exposed without the foreskin? Let us agree for a moment to take these two words—gesturing toward but never arriving at the site of trauma (the homonymic *glans*)—as a "fetish" for Freud.[8] Think of them as a "word-thing," meaning that they work analogously to such stereotypical fetishes as the high-heeled shoe or the cashmere sweater. *Glanz* and g*lance* could be read as the last critical impressions before the uncanny traumatic one of the circumcised foreskin.

It is possible to understand how the circumcised foreskin could function traumatically for Freud by considering the racializing eugenics discourses of the nineteenth century. In his book *Freud, Race, and Gender*, Sander Gilman has shown how Aryan racial discourse of the later nineteenth century regarded Jews as a degenerate mixed race, so much so that Jews were even thought to be Negroes, a categorization of utter abjection. Sexology also contributed to racializing Jews by blurring castration and circumcision and denigrating circumcision as feminizing; indeed, Gilman notes that Viennese slang called the clitoris a "Jew" and female masturbation was called "play[ing] with the Jew."[9] It constructed the clitoral glans as the unspeakable discursive limit of the circumcised foreskin.[10] This racialized epistemology produced the male Jew as an abject non-subject.[11]

Freud knew this eugenics literature and he wrote his essay on fetishism as a kind of photographic negative of eugenics discourse. Thus, for Freud, a circumcised Jew, the last discursive impression before the "uncanny traumatic one" of the clitoral *glans* would be the foreskin. The *glans*, dissimulated by Freud as *Glanz/glance*, appears then just before the recognition of the hegemonic violence of racialized and sexualized discourse regarding Jews, which circulated in Freud's Vienna. Put another way, Freud's circumcised foreskin belatedly returns as an institutional trauma, one that has to do with antisemitic discursive formations in medicine and eugenics. For Freud, a circumcised Jewish scientist who was deeply concerned precisely to institutionalize psychoanalysis as a science, and who therefore needed to do so in the dominant phantasmatic form of the "intact" Christian bourgeois male body, the characteristically Jewish/racialized/feminized *glans*, the circumcised foreskin, could only be spoken of through its untranslatability.

There are lessons to be learned from the echoes of Freud's essay. Just as institutional trauma precluded Freud from translating across and between his own historical embodiment and his scientific work, so does institutional trauma in history preclude rethinking supersession. Freud's essay on the fetish fetishistically marks the spacing in which glans and foreskin were sutured in racialist discourse. So too has historical study of the fetish worked both to periodize and institutionalize modernity as supersession.

Two important discussions of the fetish by Anne McClintock (*Imperial Leather*) and William Pietz ("The Problem of the Fetish") help to illustrate my point. In their view, the *feitiço* of the Middle Ages is simply not the true fetish, an object which they claim (as psychoanalysts do for the uncanny) emerges in early modernity. Pietz thinks of the fetish as "an idea and a problem, as a novel object not proper to any prior discrete society, originated in the cross-cultural spaces on the coast of West Africa during the sixteenth and seventeenth century."[12] He expends much energy separating the medieval notion of "fetish"— which, according to him, first appears in Iberian law in 1176 in a municipal code for Tervel in Aragon, where a section on the crimes of women (*De muliere facticiosa*) legislates against those making magical objects—from the usage of fetish by Portuguese traders among the West African tribes in the fifteenth and sixteenth centuries. Pietz carefully delineates the incommensurability of the medieval and the early modern fetish as one of economic epistemology: "the notion of the *feitiço*, as conceived within [medieval] church doctrine on witchcraft, did not raise the essential problem of the fetish: the problem of the social and personal value of material objects."[13] Pietz thus uses the fetish, his "novel subject," to sort out historical time (periodization) *and* cultural space (Europe and Africa). His economic model drops out the troubling exchange of people as objects and trinkets as things in Portuguese/West African trade. His narrow economic definition of the fetish as a material object enables him to ward off these traumatic economics of slavery. Pietz models his modern fetish as the last impression before catching sight of the enslaved African body.

McClintock thinks about the fetish more capaciously than Pietz. According to her, the fetish "stands at the cross-roads of psychoanalysis and social history, inhabiting the threshold of both personal and historical memory."[14] By opening up the fetish to a psychoanalytic register, McClintock acknowledges that the fetish can occupy several positions—magical, material, and sexual—simultaneously. Yet, surprisingly, the complexity she allows the fetish has no effect on the way she uses periodization. She begins her genealogy of imperialism conventionally with Columbus in 1492 and illustrates her point with that well-known and ubiquitously reproduced engraving of Vespucci encountering America embodied as a naked female "native."[15] She starts rethinking the fetish from the fetishized event of 1492. The periodization of *Imperial Leather*, conceived through an implicit premodernity, paradoxically repeats the imperial supersessions inherent in anthropological discourse on the fetish circulating in the nineteenth century. Take, for example, the key texts as Edward Tylor's *Primitive Culture: Researches into the Development of Mythology, Philosophy, Religion, Art and Custom* (1871) and F. Max Müller's *Lectures on the Origin and Growth of Religion* (1878). For Tylor fetishism served as the sign of the originary "primitive," the racialized, the West African, the "pre-"; for Müller, fetishisms were the sign of a "post," that which comes after the Aryan, the Aryan being in Müller's model the very condition of possibility for a past, a past racialized in the form of white religious supremacy. Black and white, pre- and post-, the fetishes of periodization and the periodizations of the fetish do read fetishistically: "I know it but even so"—I know the problem of imperial time but even so I want its periodizations. Premodernity as conventionally periodized works as the "the last impression received before the uncanny traumatic one."

The fetish of Freud and the fetish of anthropologists suggest the importance of defetishizing supersession and rethinking the fetish unhistorically. The spacing of the fetish between body and institution, between human-object and trinket-thing, offers a gap in which to start such a project. The much acclaimed postcolonial ethnography, *In an Antique Land*, with its rich verbal fetishes, provides a source for this study. Ghosh describes the Mediterranean trading diaspora of the ninth through the twelfth centuries as a medieval Golden Age. For Ghosh, this Mediterranean world is the site of history with a small "h," that is, "indistinguishable, intertwined histories, Indian, Egyptian, Hindu and Muslim."[16] By the fifteenth century, according to Ghosh, Europeans would bring to this diaspora history with a capital "H," that is, a metahistory of violence and force that permanently shattered this medieval utopia. He painstakingly constructs his Golden Age out of documentary fragments preserved from the archive of the Cairo Geniza. Ghosh gives special attention to piecing together the history of a medieval Hindu slave—discovered in the document MS H.6 of the Cairo Geniza—who served a Jewish merchant on the Malibar coast in the trading diaspora of the twelfth century. He intertwines the archival story of the slave with an ethnography of his fieldwork undertaken in peasant villages in Egypt in the 1980s.

As in recent histories of the fetish by Pietz and McClintock, Ghosh imagines an impassable divide between premodernity (history with a small "h") and modernity (history with a large "H"). There are body parts (namely foreskin, clitoris, and testicles), however, that haunt his text and transgress the binary he would maintain. Ghosh's impossible desire for a plenitudinous medieval Golden Age gets written back on him, we shall see, as these severed genitalia. As in my reading of Freud's essay on fetishism, I am curious to mark which translations Ghosh avoids in a work that is all about translation. His refusals to translate become for me the clues to sites of historiographic trauma that remain unthought, these sites that can help us to understand the institutional dispossessions that are too traumatic for Ghosh to avow.

Words Are the Thing

From the outset words are trouble in *In an Antique Land*; they are not what they seem. At crucial moments of ethnographic encounter, Ghosh cannot find the words for things. The very first word to fail Ghosh in his ethnography is the word for "sex." Soon after his arrival in the Egyptian village of Lataifa he describes himself in the fascinated act of watching a pair of ducks mating. He writes: "I had no conception that ducks had penises and vaginas."[17] A young villager named Jabir has been watching Ghosh's fascination with the mating scene and proceeds to ask, "What do you know on the subject of . . . "[18] Ghosh does not recognize Jabir's colloquial Arabic for "sex" and has to look it up afterward in the dictionary. His ignorance is the cause of adolescent hilarity to Jabir, who quickly veers the conversation to the question of circumcision. For the first time Ghosh reveals to a villager the fact that he is not circumcised. Where there had been a failure of translation around sex, Ghosh now suddenly supplies an abundance of knowledge, an etymology for the word circumcision: "In Arabic the word 'circumcise' derives from the root that means 'to purify': to say of someone that they are 'uncircumcised' is more or less to call them impure."[19]

Foreskins hover around the ethnography and return again in its second section where Ghosh describes the most probing discussion of circumcision to occur between him and the villagers. Here is the exchange:

> "So what about circumcision?" a voice demanded, and was followed immediately by another, even louder one, which wanted to know whether women in my country were "purified" as they were in Egypt. The word to "purify" makes a verbal equation between male circumcision and clitoridectomy, being the same in both cases, but the latter is an infinitely more dangerous operation, since it requires the complete excision of the clitoris.[20]

So insistent are the villagers that an anguished Ghosh abruptly leaves the conversation. How can he reconcile his corporeal "wholeness"—his intact foreskin that seemingly guarantees immunity from castration—with its "impurity"—the foreskin being the analogue to the clitoris among the villagers?[21] By virtue of his intact foreskin, Ghosh becomes paradoxically a dirty woman, an uncircumcised woman with a clitoris, a castrated, *but not castrated enough*, figure. Ghosh is faced with the fantastic dilemma of having it (the phallus) and being it (the clitoris). Rather than explore the unhistorical possibilities of rethinking the embodiment of the ethnographer, rather than explore the crisscrossings of identification and desire inherent in his dilemma, and rather than explore the gap in between the foreskin and the clitoris, Ghosh, instead, disavows the paradoxes of his fieldwork through his use of history. He anxiously insists on the temporal binary of history with a small "h"—his Golden Age—and a capital "H"—the violence of Europe—as operating fetishistically to keep these lines of desire/identification on the straight and narrow. In so doing, as I shall now show, he misses the violence (with a small "v") within his golden history.

The Scene of the Accident

There is another body part, the testicle, which produces gaps in Ghosh's efforts to keep temporality and corporeality on the straight and narrow in *In an Antique Land.*

I take up his ethnography again as Ghosh travels to the Malibar coast to conduct the philological research necessary to decipher the paleography of the slave's name that appears in document MS H.6: "For me a great deal depended on this meeting, for my unraveling of the slave's history had been blocked by an intractable etymological puzzle, the mystery of his name."[22] The slave of MS H.6, according to Ghosh, becomes a historical subject at the moment of archival naming: "It was thus that Bomma [the name of the slave] finally came of age and was ready at last to become a protagonist of his own story."[23]

Ghosh does not consider whether the agency of the slave as a historical subject could be constrained by his condition of enslavement. In the tension between agency and subjection lies the trauma of Ghosh's own materialization as ethnographer and archivist. At this juncture in his story, Ghosh turns to the issue of slavery in the Geniza Golden Age. He compares medieval slavery to the yardstick of early modern plantation systems. Suggesting that, by comparison, medieval slavery "lacks" the modern notion of servitude and freedom, Ghosh prohibits a reading of the Enlightenment master-slave relationship back onto the Geniza trade diaspora. Slavery too has its supersessions. He claims that slavery in the lifetime of Ben Yiju, the master, and Bomma, the slave, could frequently serve as a career opening to the highest level of government and a fictive way of creating kinship. Sufi poetry written during the twelfth century imagines slavery as the "practical embodiment of perfect freedom."[24] Thus, for Ghosh, slavery during the Golden Age did not demean, but produced links "that were in some small way ennobling—human connections, pledges of commitment, in relationships that could just as well have been a matter of mere exchange of coinage."[25]

Uneasiness about the nature of slavery during this Golden Age vexes not only Ghosh but also an exemplary early revisionist work on the Geniza Golden Age written by S. D. Goitein.[26] Goitein's study, *Jews and Arabs: Their Contacts Through the Ages,* also stumbles on the question of medieval slavery. Goitein, a Zionist who left Germany in 1923 for Palestine, wrote *Jews and Arabs* for an American audience, during the period of the formation of the Israeli state after World War II. Goitein wished to trace a history of tolerant contact between Jews and Arabs that could serve as a model for future relations in the Middle East. He rejects essentialist, racialist explanations for a Semitic affinity between Jews and Arabs and instead bases their commonality on their shared history of "primitive democracy."[27]

This common democratic bond might, of course, provide a past for mapping the future of the "modern" state in the Middle East, but the historical presence of slavery jars the multicultural benignity of Goitein's wished-for Golden Age.[28] To prevent such trouble from disrupting the proleptic Enlightenment past constructed in this Golden Age by both Goitein and Ghosh, slavery has to become a family affair:

Now, slavery in the ancient East is a very complicated subject. But, when we confine ourselves to the status of slaves in Israel and in Arabia, a comparatively consistent picture emerges. There, slaves were not the wretched, sweating beasts of the American plantation, or the Roman latifundia, or the potteries of Athens; they were the members of the household with more independent status at times than sons or younger brothers.[29]

Slavery is thus a family affair and also a masculine matter. Both Ghosh and Goitein elide slavery with male, domestic slavery. The desire for a Golden Age traps them into dismissing the pervasive evidence for a large-scale, not so easily domesticated, institutionalized slavery in the military-bureaucratic sectors of the Geniza world, and they write off a large number of slaves as constituting a "barbarian slave corps,"[30] neither Arab nor Jewish, that therefore does not count in discussions of the Golden Age. The essentialist, racialist lines that Goitein eschews when he wishes to draw affinities between Jews and Arabs become the very grounds for excluding barbarian slaves. Many histories of medieval world economies likewise are silent about slavery in this Golden Age.[31] Janet Abu-Lughod, in her study *Before European Hegemony: The World System, AD 1250–1350*, simply does not acknowledge the scale of economic exchange during the ninth to the twelfth centuries and the importance of the slave trade to that exchange. Likewise, Philip Curtin, in his otherwise comprehensive *Cross-Cultural Trade in World History*, is silent about the kind of commerce that fueled the acknowledged dominance of the Mediterranean economy during this Golden Age, treating Islam as "civilization" and transmitter of "culture," but not as involved in economic exchange:

In the broadest perspective of Afro-Eurasian history, in the period from 750 AD to at least 1500, Islam was the central civilization for the whole of the Old World. Not only was it the most dynamic and creative of Rome's and Persia's successors; it was also the principal agency for contact between the discrete cultures of this period, serving as the carrier that transmitted innovations from one society to another.[32]

Revisionist archaeology too is silent about the slave trade. Richard Hodges and David Whitehouse, in their reinterpretation of the

Pirenne thesis, acknowledge a dynamic Mediterranean world economy at the moment Pirenne would argue for its blockade and collapse, but, nevertheless, these archaeologists never discuss the specificity of the exchange which materialized the abundant numismatic evidence and the lavish scale of Abbasid urban development in the Fertile Crescent and Indian Ocean.[33]

This strange silence and uneasiness about slavery in the Mediterranean Golden Age of the ninth to the twelfth centuries is troubling. Few revisionist histories seem eager to explore further the claim, made some time ago by Maurice Lombard, that long-distance slave-exchange was the very edifice that sustained the Golden Age: "slave-traffic was, then, of the utmost commercial importance."[34] To exemplify Lombard's thesis on the centrality of slave-exchange, let me conjure for you the schematic maps that he uses to illustrate the medieval pan-European-Mediterranean-Indian slave trade. He chose the symbol of the scissor to mark the border sites at which he had found evidence that slaves were castrated in preparation for their trade into the Mediterranean heartland of the Golden Age economy.

Here I wish to join the symbol of the scissors and the name of the Hindu slave, Bomma, produced by Ghosh's archival research. The word that cannot be said in the cryptonomy of Ghosh's book, the translation that cannot be made, is *not* the painstakingly reconstructed name, "Bomma," but rather, I contend, the word "slave," a word with a traveling history. The very name of slavery has a material, embodied genealogy in the long-distance exchange conducted by and across "pagan," Christian, Islamic, and Jewish trading partners during the Golden Age. Just as Freud could not say *glans*, Ghosh cannot say *slave*. The Arabic word for slave—"saqlabi" (singular) or "saqaliba" (plural)—continues in a new status designation the once ethnic designator "Slav." During the Golden Age *saqaliba* referred to those slaves originating in the Bilad as-Saqaliba, or slave country. *Saqlabi* also served as a common synonym in Arabic for the word "eunuch."[35] As early as the ninth century, reference is found to Slavic eunuchs serving as interpreters for Viking merchants in Baghdad. Adult males exchanged from Slavic regions into al-Andalus and the eastern Mediterranean were commonly castrated at ports of entry; hence, the scissors that mark these sites on Lombard's maps. The slippage from ethnic designator to status designator is a border phenomenon occurring over the ninth to tenth centuries in the border zones of the peoples of the Book, ranging from the Balkans to al-Andalus.

Not all male slaves were castrated, but the slide between *saqlabi*/slave and *saqlabi*/eunuch marks a traveling sexual trauma. This slippage brings the cryptonomy of Ghosh's book to a sexual turn. When he writes about the Sufi tradition that drew upon slavery as a spiritual metaphor, Ghosh tells an exemplary story of the Sultan Mahmud of Ghazni, who built an empire in central Asia. At a crucial moment of conquest, so the story goes, when the Sultan seemed abandoned by his troops, his slave, Ayaz, stepped into his shadow. Among Sufis this perfect act of love works a miraculous spiritual transformation and the world-conquering Mahmud becomes "the slave of his slave."[36] Other popular versions of this story celebrate Ayaz as a "catamite."[37] In Ghosh's retelling he elides the homoerotic content of the story. Not only is the violence of slave trade occluded, its homoeroticism is spiritualized. Goitein, too, is uneasy about homoeroticism. In his *Jews and Arabs*, he remarks that one of the traditions that creates a "deep gulf" between Jews and Arabs is the Arab regard for friendship, "and more than friendship," between members of the male sex as the "acme of civilization."[38] Goitein thinks that this tradition contributes to a "nervous, unbalanced state of mind in the urban population of the Arab East."[39]

The so-called "bourgeois revolution" bonding the Geniza merchant-society at its cosmpolitan center relies, I argue, on dismemberment at the borders (castration was forbidden under Islamic law).[40] Dismemberment involves not only the removal of the testicles of adolescent and adult males, but the excision of enslaved women from their communities to join "fictive families" in Cordoba, Cairo, Aden, and Mangalore. If slavery proved banal at the center—domestic and bureaucratic, a matter of family and statecraft—it was because the violence that fueled the lucrative exchange lay far away at the borders. Slaves were already DOA, "dismembered on arrival."

The slave of MS H.6 reminds us that the history of this world-economy and slave system still remains to be written. What the peoples of the Book accomplished with castration, the Enlightenment would achieve with the "universal" law of property rights—which extended to slaves as objects.[41] The breaks that Ghosh and Goitein would mark between medieval slavery and the plantation systems of the early modern period and the Enlightenment, are, I think, a misrecognition based on, and maintaining, a deeply abiding supersession that chooses not to look at the shifting border histories of the ninth through the twelfth centuries from Europe to the Indian Ocean.[42]

Fundamental Trauma

My practice of sounding out the words of trauma in Ghosh's book aims contestably at the production of a different kind of history. I tried to show what is at stake in Ghosh's periodization of a medieval Golden Age superseded by modern colonialism. I now wish to turn to a parallel track of Ghosh's ethnography, that is his grappling with contemporary politics in Egypt and the wider eastern Mediterranean. A notion of supersession shapes this contemporary material of the "this is now" just as problematically as it shaped his story of the Golden Age ("that was then"). I shall argue that such supersessionary notions stand in for his intended critique of contemporary fundamentalisms at the same time that they deny the possibility of his allowing histories to these fundamentalisms.

To tell this story of proleptic supersession, let us travel with Ghosh when, in the summer of 1990 on his way to sleuth down the name of Bomma, he paid a visit to a fishing village located on the sand-spit directly across the lagoon from Mangalore's old port. The fishing caste of the village, the Magavira, played an important historical role in Geniza Indian Ocean trade. Ghosh notices that this prosperous village has drifted away from its Tulanid tradition of Bhuta worship, in which the name "Bomma" was given to a leading god of the pantheon. Instead, the village has embraced Hinduism and built a modern temple, on which are plastered the posters of an anti-Muslim, fundamentalist Hindu political organization. Ghosh conjectures that the village is in the process of appropriating Hinduism, especially its fundamentalist modalities, to build for itself a new future. Yet Ghosh's condemnation of contemporary fundamentalisms in *In an Antique Land* cannot be separated from his affective project of producing a medieval Golden Age. To support this assertion, it is necessary to situate Ghosh as subject to and included in a tradition of Indian historiography. The desire to use the Middle Ages as an origin might be expected to have *less* affective resonance in the construction of postcolonial nationalisms in Africa, Asia, and the Middle East than it does in Europe. Not so. In a collection of brilliant essays on Indian historiography, Partha Chatterjee has shown how Indian history writing in the nineteenth century reproduced the dominant Western model of periodization—classical, medieval, renaissance. Chatterjee alerts medievalists to the remapping of medievalisms beyond conventional European borders:

> For Indian nationalists in the late nineteenth century, the pattern of glory, medieval decline, and modern renaissance appeared as one that was not only proclaimed by the modern historiography of Europe but also approved for India by at least some sections of European scholarship. What was needed was to claim for the Indian nation the historical agency for completing the project of modernity. To make that claim, ancient India had to become the

classical source of Indian modernity, while "the Muslim period" would become the night of medieval darkness.[43]

To produce the period of a medieval "dark ages" in conformity with European periodizations, Indian historiography constructed Muslim rule in India as the Dark Age, so that Islam became the excluded term of Indian historiography. Chatterjee draws important links between this historiographic tradition and the politics of contemporary fundamentalisms:

> what, we may ask, is the place of those inhabitants of India who are excluded from this nation? There are several answers suggested in this historiography. One, which assumes the centrality of the modern state in the life of the nation, is frankly majoritarian. The majority "community" is Hindu; the others are minorities. State policy must therefore reflect this preponderance, and the minorities must accept the leadership and protection of the majority. This view, which today is being propagated with such vehemence in postcolonial India by Hindu-extremist politics, actually originated more than a hundred years ago, at the same time Indian nationalism was born.[44]

The fundamentalisms, Islamic and Hindu, that Ghosh bemoans are not an aberration of the late twentieth century, but rather the Enlightenment effect of an "entirely modern, rationalist and historicist idea"[45] emplotted into Indian historiography a century ago. By denying a specific history to Hindu fundamentalism, or what Ghosh would term history with a small "h," he unwittingly contributes, via his construction of a Golden Age, to an abiding neoimperialist project that would classicize the Islamic tradition which had been excluded from Indian historiography. By classicizing this excluded Islam through a model of freedom and tolerance, the characteristics of the medieval Geniza world, Ghosh makes Islam assimilable into contemporary historiography in such a way that no one has to account for its exclusion to a "dark ages" in the first place.

Ghosh's supersession is also haunted by Jews, Ben Yiju the Jewish merchant notwithstanding. The periodization of his ethnography, shaped as it is by notions of supersession, also enables him to disregard the virtual absence of Jews from the contemporary story of his Egyptian fieldwork. Jews belong to his premodern trading diaspora. Their fate in twentieth-century Egypt goes unmentioned. Relevant to Ghosh's study is the memoir (*Out of Egypt: A Memoir*) by his contemporary André Aciman. It appeared a year after the publication of *In an Antique Land*. Aciman recalls his Jewish childhood during the Suez war and the diasporic vicissitudes of his family history in the 1960s and after.

Unhistorical Dispossession

So far in this chapter I have attempted to open up some gaps in the fetishization of supersession. In the moment in between "the last impression received before the uncanny traumatic one" unhistorical histories emerge. These unhistories have told us about the intertwining of the male Jew and the black clitoris in Freud's Vienna, about the excising of body parts of the medieval Mediterranean slave trade, and about emplotting Muslim rule in India as a Dark Age, and the twentieth-century history of Jews in Egypt.

The question remains how these unhistorical histories help us to historicize postcolonialties, that is, the fetishized corporeal organizations of archivist, fieldworker, historian, analyst in a supposed post-supersessionary world. How can we imagine unhistorical alternatives to the straight and narrow of authoritative embodiments that we have fabricated for intellectual workers? My own reimaginings follow several byways, one being Teresa de Lauretis's rereading of castration and the fetish. Her work is crucial for considering the temporal gap of the Freudian fetish, that moment between "the last impression received before the uncanny traumatic one." She exposes how that gap has been imagined temporally through the heterosexual normativity of Freud's account of desire. Freud tells the time of the fetish in terms of the developmental model of the oedipal stage. The fetish marks for Freud the "before" of sexual development. The fetishist remains in the "before"of the story. Freud's fetish is thus intrinsically linked with narrative of temporal origin—"before" and "after." Scholars have repeated this narrative in their efforts to historicize the fetish whether it be imagined materially (Pietz) or psychoanalytically (McClintock).

In a brilliant move, de Lauretis reads that temporal gap instead through Freud's negative theory, through perversion. Perversion opens up temporalities not organized by "before" and "after." She proposes that we rethink the fetish, not as Freud would have it, as detachment from the penile representation of the phallus, but rather as detachment from the phallus itself. The phallus then is no longer the only measure of loss nor the only moment of its timing. De Lauretis thus opens up the possibilities for considering other kinds of losses that set in motion other kinds of desires. Her specific discussion of lesbian desire argues for the loss of the female body as another modality of original loss.[46] She does not, however, essentialize the female body in the way that conventional castration theory has essentialized the phallus as the penis. She insists that the loss of the female body is the loss of an "entirely fantasmatic object"[47] of which there is no perceptual memory. The loss is a sign that marks itself on the body as a fetishistic trace. At this step in her argument De Lauretis raises crucial issues relevant to our project of imagining a temporality which is not one. Her perverse reading of the fetish in lesbian sexuality refuses the notion of an originary moment when an object was lost. She rethinks the temporality of the fetish as temporality set in motion in the *contact* of fetishes, in the *encounter* of traces, where there are two in contiguity, creating new surfaces, new temporalities. Thus temporality is relational in the desire of desire. To phrase this in another way, De Lauretis disrupts fetishistic theories of supersessionary temporality in which temporality has a founding object in the "before" and "after."

The difference between Freud's fetish and de Lauretis's perverse fetish can be shown if we return to Ghosh's ethnography. As I suggested earlier, Ghosh is not castrated enough in *In an Antique Land.* He remains attached to the privileged object of the phallus and he thus misses an unhistorical history for his slave Bomma. To render unhistorical Freud's essay on the fetish is to retranslate the corporeal materialization of the observer, be it Freud, Ghosh, the reader, or the writer of this chapter. The gap of the fetish, that temporal moment in between the "last impression" and the "trauma," need not be read as "before" and "after." That moment can be experienced instead as new temporal folds of contiguity in which traces and scars, foreskin and heart, touch within a temporality that is not one.

Notes

Introduction: Typology Never Lets Go

1. Since such supersessionary substitutions are already woven into the New Testament, it means that typological or figural thinking is never merely a textual or literary problem. Christian typology is closely bound with theological imaginaries having to do with Christology and soteriology. For close studies of the shared world of exegetical practices in the late antique world, as well as an appreciation of the breaks in the theological imaginaries even within the New Testament, see the essays in *Hebrew Bible/Old Testament: The History of Its Interpretation*, vol. 1, ed. Magne Sæbø (Göttingen: Vandenhoeck and Ruprecht, 1996), especially Hans Hübner, "New Testament Interpretation of the Old Testament," 332–72.

2. Friedrich Nietzsche uses the concept of the "unhistorical" in his *On the Advantage and Disadvantage of History for Life*, trans. Peter Preuss (Indianapolis: Hackett, 1980) in order to draw attention to "thresholds" (9). The question of thresholds and passages is important in this study, since it suggests the moment in which retroactive construction is suspended, thus allowing for temporalities that are not one.

3. See Beryl Smalley, *The Study of the Bible in the Middle Ages*, 3rd ed. (Oxford: Blackwell, 1973), 214–52. For the reference to the afterlife of the *Glossa ordinaria* and, for instance, Donne's use of this schoolbook, see Smalley, 367. Philippe Buc has also emphasized the importance of the mise-en-page to this textbook in his indispensable study, *L'Ambiguïté du livre: prince, pouvoir, et peuple dans les commentaires de la bible au moyen âge* (Paris: Beauchesne, 1994). Richard and Mary Rouse and Margaret Gibson (see note 15 below for full references) emphasize that by the mid-twelfth century most of the devices of the glossed Bible were not new and that change lay in their systematic and increasingly sophisticated application. Thus, I am giving a generally formalized account and concentrating on what Smalley has described as the proceeding together of the production of textbook aids and independent exegesis (51).

4. The canonical locus for opening discussion is still Erich Auerbach's essay on "Figura," first published in *Neue Dantestudien*, Istanbuler Schriften 5 (Istanbul, 1944), and translated and printed in *Scenes from the Drama of European Literature* (Minneapolis: University of Minnesota Press, 1984), 11–76. Jon Whitman notes the doubleness of typological thinking and the conflicts it created in the early church in his study *Allegory: The Dynamics of an Ancient and Medieval Technique* (Cambridge, Mass.: Harvard University Press, 1987), 68. Also see his edited collection: *Interpretation and Allegory: Antiquity to the*

Modern Period (Leiden: Brill, 2000). For a more celebratory recognition of the force of figural realism, see Hayden White, "Auerbach's Literary History: Figural Causation and Modernist Historicism," in *Figural Realism: Studies in the Mimesis Effect* (Baltimore: Johns Hopkins University Press, 1999), 87–100. In his *Political Unconscious: Narrative as a Socially Symbolic Act* (Ithaca, N.Y.: Cornell University Press, 1981), Fredric Jameson conceives of his Marxist criticism as the fulfillment of medieval figural thinking without analyzing how Marx himself failed to achieve a post-medieval, post-theological discourse, in spite of his claims. For an important discussion of both Auerbach and Marx see Jeffrey S. Librett, *The Rhetoric of Cultural Dialogue: Jews and Germans from Moses Mendelssohn to Richard Wagner and Beyond* (Stanford, Calif.: Stanford University Press, 2000), 12–19, 219–40. Frances M. Young in her *Biblical Exegesis and the Formation of Christian Culture* (Cambridge: Cambridge University Press, 1997) reconsiders allegory and typology in early Christian hermeneutics and refuses to separate allegory from typology. The anxious insistence on a sharp divide between typology and allegory is, I think, a way of warding off anxiety about the excess of typology. For revival of typological studies after World War II see Henri de Lubac, *Medieval Exegesis: The Four Senses of Scripture*, trans. E. M. Macierowski (Grand Rapids, Michigan: Eerdmans, 2000) a translation of de Lubac's *Exégèse médiévale: les quatre sens de l'Écriture* (Paris: Aubier, 1959). Daniel Boyarin has much to say about allegory that contradicts Auerbach's sharp separation between allegory and figural thinking in his *Radical Jew: Paul and the Politics of Identity* (Berkeley: University of California Press, 1994). He summarizes his argument in "'This We Know to be the Carnal Israel': Circumcision and the Erotic Life of God and Israel," *Critical Inquiry* 18 (1992): 474–503.

5. My work is indebted to Eric L. Santner, *On the Psychotheology of Everyday Life: Reflections on Freud and Rosenzweig* (Chicago: University of Chicago Press, 2001), 26. I am also attempting to theorize links between graphic technologies and concepts of embodiment along the lines suggested by Mark Hansen, *Embodying Technesis: Technology Beyond Writing* (Ann Arbor: University of Michigan Press, 2000).

6. For a useful summary of recent papal statements and an important examination of how typology plays out in contemporary theological textbooks see Philip A. Cunningham, *Education for Shalom: Religion Textbooks and the Enhancement of the Catholic and Jewish Relationship* (Collegeville, Minn.: Liturgical Press, 1995), especially 44, 141. The text of the Commission for Religious Relations with the Jews: Notes on the Correct Way to Present the Jews and Judaism in Preaching and Catechesis in the Roman Catholic Church, June 1985, may be found in *More Stepping Stones to Jewish Christian Relations*, compiled by Helga Croner (Mahwah, N.J.: Paulist Press, 1985), 220–32; citation 224.

7. Robert E. Lerner, *The Feast of Saint Abraham: Medieval Millenarians and the Jews* (Philadelphia: University of Pennsylvania Press, 2001), 19.

8. Joseph Blenkinsopp, "Tanakh and the New Testament: A Christian Perspective," in *Biblical Studies: Meeting Ground of Jews and Christians*, ed. Lawrence Boadt, Helga Croner, and Leon Klenicki (New York: Paulist Press, 1980), 113.

9. Robert Moore, *The Formation of a Persecuting Society: Power and Deviance in Western Europe, 950–1250* (Oxford: Blackwell, 1987). For a perspective on the relation of Moore's work to studies of Jewish-Christian relations see Anna Sapir Abulafia, "From Northern Europe to Southern Europe and from the

General to the Particular: Recent Research on Jewish-Christian Coexistence in Medieval Europe," *Journal of Medieval History* 23 (1997): 179–90; also Robert Moore, "Anti-Semitism and the Birth of Europe," in *Christianity and Judaism*, ed. Diana Wood, Studies in Church History 29 (Oxford: Blackwell, 1992); 33–57.

10. Gavin Langmuir, *History, Religion, and Antisemitism* (Berkeley: University of California Press, 1990); idem, *Toward a Definition of Antisemitism* (Berkeley: University of California Press, 1990). Langmuir defines antisemitism as "an irrational reaction to repressed rational doubts (*History, Religion, and Antisemitism*, 276). For a thoughtful review of Langmuir's important studies, see Robert C. Stacey, "History, Religion, and Medieval Antisemitism: A Response to Gavin Langmuir," *Religious Studies Review* 20 (1994): 95–101; and Anna Sapir Abulafia, *Christians and Jews in the Twelfth-Century Renaissance* (New York: Routledge, 1995).

11. Jeremy Cohen, *Living Letters of the Law: Ideas of the Jew in Medieval Christianity* (Berkeley: University of California Press, 1999). Cohen relies strongly on the magisterial work of Amos Funkenstein, *Perceptions of Jewish History* (Berkeley: University of California Press, 1993). It should be noted that Funkenstein does not take up Moore's thesis. His study addresses the work of Yosef Hayim Yerushalmi, *Zakhor: Jewish History and Jewish Memory* (Seattle: University of Washington Press, 1982) and questions Yerushalmi's opposition of collective memory to historiography. In his monumental *Les Intellectuels chrétiens et les Juifs au moyen âge* (Paris: Éditions du Cerf, 1990), Gilbert Dahan does not problematize the imaginary of Christian-Jewish relations. Stacey points out the typological conundrum of Langmuir's work ("History, Religion, and Medieval Antisemitism," 97).

12. Julia Reinhard Lupton, *Afterlives of the Saints: Hagiography, Typology, and Renaissance Literature* (Stanford, Calif.: Stanford University Press, 1996), 23. I only broach the very complicated question of Islam and the Koran in the Christian typological imaginary in Chapter 5. Jeremy Cohen frames the problem, "The Muslim Connection: On the Changing Role of the Jew in High Medieval Theology," in *From Witness to Witchcraft: Jews and Judaism in Medieval Christian Thought* (Wiesbaden: Harrassowitz Verlag, 1996), 141–63. Islamic theological notions of supersession and scriptural exegesis in relation to Christian concepts of supersession are in need of comparative study. See Hava Lazarus-Yafeh, *Intertwined Worlds: Medieval Islam and Bible Criticism* (Princeton, N.J.: Princeton University Press, 1992); and Camilla Adang, *Muslim Writers on Judaism and the Hebrew Bible* (New York: Brill, 1996).

13. David Nirenberg, *Communities of Violence: Persecution of Minorities in the Middle Ages* (Princeton, N.J.: Princeton University Press, 1996), 5. Context becomes problematic in Nirenberg's study, since he refuses to allow the possibility that context is always already discursive. He relies instead on a positivist notion of context as specific time and place and cannot account for the work of the kinds of narratives studied by Miri Rubin in her *Gentile Tales: The Narrative Assault on Late Medieval Jews* (New Haven, Conn.: Yale University Press, 1999), 28.

14. Sara Lipton, *Images of Intolerance: The Representation of Jews and Judaism in the Bible moralisée* (Berkeley: University of California Press, 1999). For her discussion of Moore see 51–52; citation 53. Her work is cogently supplemented by Katherine H. Tachau, "God's Compass and Vana Curiositas: Scientific Study in the Old French Bible Moralisée," *Art Bulletin* 89 (1998): 8–33; and by

John Lowden, *The Making of the Bibles Moralisées*, 2 vols. (University Park: Pennsylvania State University Press, 2000).

15. Christopher de Hamel, *Glossed Books of the Bible and the Origins of the Paris Book Trade* (Dover, N.H.: D.S. Brewer, 1984), 24; Richard H. Rouse and Mary A. Rouse, "Statim invenire: Schools, Preachers, and New Attitudes to the Page," in *Renaissance and Renewal in the Twelfth Century*, ed. Robert L. Benson and Giles Constable (Toronto: University of Toronto Press, 1982), 210–28; John Van Engen, "Studying Scripture in the Early University," in *Neue Richtungen in der hoch-und spätmittelalterlichen Bibelexegese*, ed. Robert. E. Lerner, Schriften des Historischen Kolleges Kolloquien 32 (Munich: R. Oldenbourg Verlag, 1996), 17–38; Michael A. Signer, "The Glossa Ordinaria and the Transmission of Medieval Anti-Judaism," in *A Distinct Voice: Medieval Studies in Honor of Leonard E. Boyle, O.P.*, ed. Jacqueline Brown and William P. Stoneman (Notre Dame, Ind.: University of Notre Dame Press, 1997), 591–605. I am aware of debates over de Hamel's study but remain interested in the overall formal aspects of the modular layout he is able to isolate. For criticisms of de Hamel's study, see Theresa Gross-Diaz, *The Psalms Commentary of Gilbert of Poitiers: From Lectio Divina to the Lecture Room* (New York: Brill, 1996); reviews of his book by Patricia Stirnemann in *Bulletin Monumental* 143 (1985): 363–67; and by Margaret T. Gibson in *The Library: Transactions of the Bibliographical Society* 8 (1986): 166–69; and further by Stirnemann, "Où ont été fabriqués les livres de la Glose ordinaire dans la première moitié du XII siècle," in *Le XIIᵉ siècle: mutations et renouveau en France dans la première moitié du XII siècle*, ed. Françoise Gasparri (Paris: Léopard d'Or, 1994), 257–301.

16. Gloss text and Bible text were distinguished paleographically by their script. The script of the gloss retains its early twelfth-century form and goes on to become an independent script in its own right used for classical texts, and even as the script for the small, portable, one-volume Bibles that become popular in the late twelfth century. The display script for the biblical text becomes the liturgical display hand of the gothic period. Biblical books glossed by Peter Lombard (Epistles, Psalms) tended to lose their interlinear glosses.

17. Medieval scholars working on the glossed Bible have realized the significance of this graphic operation, yet discursive studies of inscription have tended to skip over its transformative capacities. Ivan Illich has isolated its importance in his study of how texts become detached from the physical reality of the modular page. My concern is how the "physical reality of the page" gets constituted as a chief organizing framework for information. See Ivan Illich, *ABC: The Alphabetization of the Popular Mind* (New York: Vintage Books, 1988); and *In the Vineyard of the Text: A Commentary to Hugh's Didascalicon* (Chicago: University of Chicago Press, 1993). The period 1140–70 saw an avalanche in the production of glossed Bible manuscripts. The word "avalanche" comes from Margaret T. Gibson, "The Twelfth-Century Glossed Bibles," *Studia Patristica* 23 (1989): 241, rpt. in Gibson, *"Artes" and Bible in the Medieval West* (Aldershot: Variorum, 1993); Margaret Gibson and Karlfried Froehlich, *Biblia latina cum Glossa ordinaria*, facsimile ed. (Turnhout: Brepols, 1992). The following references offer an exemplary but not exhaustive guide to study of the glossed Bible as a physical artifact: Smalley, *Study of the Bible in the Middle Ages*; Buc, *L'Ambiguïté du livre*; Gross-Diaz, *The Psalms Commentary of Gilbert of Poitiers*; Gilbert Dahan, *L'Éxégèse chrétienne de la Bible en occident médiéval (XII–XIV siècle)* (Paris: Éditions du Cerf, 1999) and his essay "Genres,

Forms and Various Methods in Christian Exegesis of the Middle Ages," in *Hebrew Bible/Old Testament*, 196–236; also in the same volume see Rainer Berndt, "The School of St. Victor in Paris," 467–96.

18. De Hamel discusses the changing apprehension of the Bible as a physical artifact (12). His discussion of the changing layout of the pages of glossed biblical texts occurs in Chapter 2 (14–27). What I am describing predates the rendering of the Bible as a "university" artifact replete with the protocols of "instant access," such as alphabetical indexing, concordances etc. See Rouse, "Statim invenire."

19. A recent study, Timothy K. Beal and David M. Gunn, eds., *Reading Bibles, Writing Bodies: Identity and the Book* (New York: Routledge, 1997), surprised me in that it does not address in any detail the changing epistemology or technology of the Bible as book.

20. The woodcut, widely reproduced, appeared in Durer's *Unterweysung der Messung* (1538) reproduced in Dürer, *Schriftlicher Nachlass*, ed. Hans Rupprich, vol. 2 (Berlin: Deutscher Verein für Kunstwissenschaft, 1966), 391. Hubert Damisch discusses this device in his reevaluation of the history of perspective, *The Origin of Perspective*, trans. John Goodman (Cambridge, Mass.: MIT Press, 1994).

21. The Old French *Bible moralisée* can be consulted in two facsimiles: Reiner Haussherr, *Bible moralisée: Faksimile-Ausgabe im Original-format des Codex Vindobonensis 2554 der Österreichischen Nationalbibliothek*, 2 vols. (Graz: Akademischer Druck, 1992); Gerald B. Guest, *Bible moralisée: Codex Vindobonensis 2554, Vienna, Österreichische Nationalbibliothek* (London: Harvey Miller, 1995). Scholars debate their dating. Tachau dates the Old French version first and earliest (1208–1215). It now seems agreed that the Latin version followed the Old French in the 1220s. Lowden devotes comparative analysis to the book of Ruth in his *Making of the Bibles Moralisées*.

22. Lipton carefully examines the political and cultural context for these two manuscripts, drawing on William Chester Jordan, *The French Monarchy and the Jews: From Philip Augustus to the Last Capetians* (Philadelphia: University of Pennsylvania Press, 1989).

23. Lipton, *Images*, 163, n. 48. Curiously enough, the illustration program, which was laid out first, represses the problem of circumcision by skipping over Genesis 17, in which God commands the covenant of circumcision.

24. Walter Benjamin, *The Origins of German Tragic Drama*, trans. John Osborne (New York: Verso, 1977), 176–83, citation 178. The work of Walter Benjamin on baroque allegory and its affinities with medieval thinking is suggestive: "In the ruin history has physically merged into the setting. And in this guise history does not assume the form of the process of an eternal life so much as that of irresistible decay."

25. My colleagues John Van Engen and Michael A. Signer draw our attention to anxiety in the introduction and conclusion to their edited collection on *Jews and Christians in Twelfth-Century Europe* (Notre Dame, Ind.: University of Notre Dame Press, 2001). See also Boyarin, *Radical Jew*, for extensive discussion and the following essay for specific philological considerations: Joel Marcus, "The Circumcision and the Uncircumcision in Rome," *New Testament Studies* 35 (1989): 67–81.

26. Daniel Boyarin, in *Radical Jew*, has anticipated the crux of the issue at stake here in his discussion of the midrashic interpretation of circumcision: "The penis—not phallus—in this text constructs precisely the refusal of the logos" (37).

Chapter 1. Christians Mapping Jews

I dedicate this chapter to the memory of Lily E. Kay, friend and colleague. Sealy Gilles and Sylvia Tomasch first invited an early version of this paper in the session they organized on *Text and Territory* at the International Congress of Medieval Studies, Kalamazoo, Michigan, in May, 1995. They published that paper ("The ABC of Ptolemy: Mapping the World with the Alphabet") in their volume *Text and Territory: Geographical Imagination in the European Middle Ages* (Philadelphia: University of Pennsylvania Press, 1998). I thank them for their scrupulous and gracious editorial labors. I have rethought and updated that essay to clarify its links with the concern of this book, the Christian typological imaginary and graphic technologies.

1. Brian Stock, *Listening for the Text: On the Uses of the Past* (Baltimore: Johns Hopkins University Press, 1990), 120.

2. Bruno Latour, *We Have Never Been Modern* (Cambridge, Mass.: Harvard University Press, 1993), 76.

3. Latour, *We Have Never Been Modern*, 72.

4. Latour, *We Have Never Been Modern*, 75.

5. Talal Asad's *Genealogies of Religion* (Baltimore: Johns Hopkins University Press, 1993) guides me here.

6. J. B. Harley and David Woodward, *Cartography in Prehistoric, Ancient, and Medieval Europe and the Mediterranean*, vol. 1 of *The History of Cartography* (Chicago: University of Chicago Press, 1987), 504. In her lucid overview of medieval *mappaemundi* Evelyn Edson regards the discovery of Ptolemaic maps in the fifteenth century as "revolutionary": *Mapping Time and Space: How Medieval Mapmakers Viewed Their World* (London: British Museum Press, 1997), 165. In contrast, Patrick Gautier Dalché has recently argued (as I had done in 1995 and as I do now) against a sharp break in medieval cartography with the "rediscovery" of the *Geography* in the fifteenth century: "Le Souvenir de la Géographie de Ptolémée dans le monde latin médiéval (VI–XIV siècles)," *Euphrosyne* 27 (1999): 79–106. He also explores the "memory" of Ptolemaic coordinates in medieval mapping: "Les Coordonnées géographiques dans le moyen âge latin," in *Science antique, science médiévale,* ed. Louis Collebat and Olivier Desbordes, Autour d'Avranches 235 (New York: Olms-Weidmann, 2000), 401–35; see also his essay, "Sur 'l'originalité' de la 'géographie' médiévale" in *Auctor et auctoritas: invention et conformisme dans l'écriture médiévale,* ed. Michel Zimmermann, Mémoires et documents de l'École des Chartes (Paris: École des Chartes, 2001), 131–44. Andrew Gow, building on the presentations given at the Text and Territory session at Kalamazoo in 1995, has subsequently explored the continuities between *mappaemundi* and Ptolemaic maps of the fifteenth century in his essay "Gog and Magog on Mappaemundi and Early Printed World Maps: Orientalizing Ethnography in the Apocalyptic Tradition," *Journal of Early Modern History* 2 (1998): 61–88.

7. For a comprehensive survey of the *mappaemundi* tradition, see Marcia Kupfer, "Medieval World Maps: Embedded Images, Interpretative Frames," *Word and Image* 10 (1994): 262–88. See also the excellent chapter on *mappaemundi* in Harley and Woodward, *Cartography in Prehistoric, Ancient, and Medieval Europe and the Mediterranean* and Edson, *Mapping Time* and *Space.*

8. Johannes Fabian, *Time and the Other: How Anthropology Makes Its Objects* (New York: Columbia University Press, 1983), 31. My argument that Jews were first fabricated as the "primitives" within the Christian imaginary is indebted

to the critical ethnography of Jonathan Boyarin, "Jewish Ethnography and the Question of the Book," in *Storm from Paradise: The Politics of Jewish Memory* (Minneapolis: University of Minnesota Press, 1992), 52–76, and his essay "From Derrida to Fichte? The New Europe, the Same Europe, and the Place of the Jews," in *Thinking in Jewish* (Chicago: University of Chicago Press, 1996), 108–39.

9. I use the word "colonize" to think about systemic domination and subordination, whereby "to colonize" means to disempower psychically as well as corporeally. Sara Suleri, in *The Rhetoric of English India* (Chicago: University of Chicago Press, 1992), has called this undoing colonialism's "intimate terror." Many medievalists either reject the notion of medieval colonialism as oxymoronic, indeed anachronistic, or draw sharp differences between modern and medieval colonialism; see Robert Bartlett, *The Making of Europe: Conquest, Colonization and Cultural Change 950–1350* (Princeton, N.J.: Princeton University Press, 1993), 306–14. Such arguments frequently rely uncritically on the work of Benedict Anderson, who, in *Imagined Communities: Reflections on the Origin and Spread of Nationalism* (London: Verso, 1991), has linked colonialism with the project of nation. Such linkage is too rigid; the impulse to periodize colonialism and ethnography begins to look very different if one includes Jews. For an excellent discussion of this important point, see John M. Efron, *Defenders of the Race: Jewish Doctors and Race Science in Fin-de-Siècle Europe* (New Haven, Conn.: Yale University Press, 1994), and Daniel Boyarin, "Épater l'embourgeoisement: Freud, Gender, and the (De) Colonized Psyche," *Diacritics* 24 (1994): 17–41.

10. As he writes, "Et hoc ergo certe non abnego, tuo namque ipsius gladio occidere te multum cupio" ("I [Petrus] certainly do not deny this, for I strongly desire to kill you with your own sword," *Patrologia Latina* 15, cols. 527–62, citation 539).

11. The thorough study of Petrus Alfonsi by John Tolan, *Petrus Alfonsi and His Medieval Readers* (Gainesville: University Press of Florida, 1993) served as a chief source for me. More recently, see Charles S. F. Burnett, "The Works of Petrus Alfonsi: Questions of Authenticity," *Medium Aevum* 66 (1997): 42–79. See the following selected works for background on Christian-Jewish polemic and specifically on the polemics of Petrus Alfonsi and Gilbert Crispin: Amos Funkenstein, "Basic Types of Christian Anti-Jewish Polemics in the Later Middle Ages," *Viator* 2 (1971): 373–82; Anna Sapir Abulafia, "Jewish-Christian Disputations and the Twelfth-Century Renaissance," *Journal of Medieval History* 15 (1989): 105–25; and her "Bodies in the Jewish-Christian Debate," in *Framing Medieval Bodies*, ed. Sarah Kay and Miri Rubin (Manchester: Manchester University Press, 1994), 124–37; Gilbert Dahan, *La Polémique chrétienne contre le Judaïsme au moyen âge* (Paris: Albin Michel, 1991); and his *Les Intellectuels chrétiens et les Juifs au moyen âge* (Paris: Éditions du Cerf, 1990); Jeremy Cohen, *Living Letters of the Law: Ideas of the Jew in Medieval Christianity* (Berkeley: University of California Press, 1999); Amos Funkenstein, *Perceptions of Jewish History* (Berkeley: University of California Press, 1993); Aryeh Grabois, "The *Hebraica Veritas* and Jewish-Christian Relations in the Twelfth Century," *Speculum* 50 (1975): 613–34; and Bernhard Blumenkranz, *Disputatio Iudei et Christiani Gilberti Crispini* (Antwerp: Spectrum, 1956). The popularity of Alfonsi's polemic is attested to by the fact that it continued to be copied through the fifteenth century (twenty-one copies in the twelfth century, twenty-four in the thirteenth, fourteen in the fourteenth, eighteen in the

fifteenth). It traveled alone in only 14 percent of the instances; of the sixty-eight medieval copies bound with other material, eight or 12 percent occurred with texts of the Victorine canons.

12. Discussion of astrolabes in this section and throughout this paper relies on the following studies: George Sarton, *Introduction to the History of Science*, vol. 2, *From Rabbi Ben Ezra to Roger Bacon* (Baltimore: Williams and Wilkins for Carnegie Institution, 1931); Willy Hartner, "The Principle and Use of the Astrolabe," in *Oriens, Occidens: Ausgewählte Schriften zur Wissenschafts- und Kulturgeschichte* (Hildesheim: Georg Olms, 1968), 287–311; J. D. North, "The Astrolabe," in *Stars, Minds, and Fate: Essays in Medieval Cosmology* (New York: Hambledon, 1989), 211–21; Solomon Gandz, "The Astrolabe in Jewish Literature," in *Studies in Hebrew Astronomy and Mathematics* (New York: Ktav, 1970), 245–62; Robert William T. Gunther, *The Astrolabes of the World*, 2 vols., 3rd ed. (London: Holland Press, 1972); and his *Chaucer and Messahalla on the Astrolabe*, vol. 5 of *Early Science in Oxford* (Oxford: Oxford University Press, 1929); Peter Travis, "Chaucer's Chronographie, the Confounded Reader, and Fourteenth Century Measurements of Time," *Disputatio* 2 (1997): 1–34. The main part of the astrolabe, its inner surface, which is usually depressed to accept the thin disk inscribed with the stereographic projection for the latitude in which the astrolabe is being used, is called the "mother" ("mater" in Latin; "umm" in Arabic); see Gunther, *Chaucer and Messahalla on the Astrolabe*, for text and illustrations of Chaucer's *Treatise on the Astrolabe*. The first Latin account of the astrolabe appears in *De mensura astrolabii* (1040) by Hermann Contractus, a pupil of the monastery school of Reichenau (see Hartner, 290), to be followed by Adelard of Bath's treatise c.1142–46 (see Sarton, *Introduction to the History of Science*, vol. 2, 1668). Also relevant is Raymond Mercier, "Astronomical Tables in the Twelfth Century," in *Adelard of Bath: An English Scientist and Arabist of the Early Twelfth Century*, ed. Charles S. F. Burnett (London: Warburg Institute, 1987), 87–118.

13. In addition to references to astrolabes in above, see also Y. Tzvi Langermann, *The Jews and the Sciences in the Middle Ages* (Brookfield, Vt.: Ashgate, 1999); Ron Barkai, "L'Astrologie juive médiévale: aspects théoriques et pratiques," *Le Moyen Âge* 43 (1987): 323–48; Raphael Levy, *The Astrological Works of Abraham Ibn Ezra*, Johns Hopkins Studies in Romance Literatures and Languages 8 (Baltimore: Johns Hopkins University Press, 1927); Bernard R. Goldstein, "The Survival of Arabic Astronomy in Hebrew," *Theory and Observation in Ancient and Medieval Astronomy*, article 21 (London: Variorum, 1985), and his "The Hebrew Astrolabe in the Adler Planetarium," article 18. The earliest surviving astrolabe, already highly evolved, dates to 984. I am interested in the proliferation of astrolabes after this date in crosscultural spaces of Islamic-Christian-Jewish contact. Gunther describes six astrolabes from the eleventh century. Surviving Jewish astrolabes (inscribed with Hebrew lettering) postdate the twelfth century; see Gunther, *Astrolabes of the World*, 302–4.

14. Alfonsi himself is not known to have written a treatise on the astrolabe, but his English student, Walcher of Malvern, used the astrolabe, and another, Adelard of Bath, wrote a treatise on its use; see Tolan, *Petrus Alfonsi*, 42, 47.

15. Alfonsi, "Dialogia," 157: 567.

16. My thoughts about the fetish here are inspired by Teresa de Lauretis's rethinking of the fetish as dispossession in *The Practice of Love: Lesbian Sexuality and Perverse Desire* (Bloomington: Indiana University Press, 1993). See further in Chapter 5. The technologies I am discussing dispossess and in so

doing become fetish effigies "with no past and no future" (266). Where they differ from the practice of love described by de Lauretis, the desire for the desire of the other (251), is in their claim to render material an object that the typological imaginary has disincarnated. Through disincarnation of historical subjects, these technologies pretend to incarnate the "real" as object. This uncanny dispossession of identity accomplished by Alfonsi in his polemical astronomy lesson can also be read as a powerful moment of "internal colonization" of the Jews in medieval Christendom. He uses science and logic first to stratify knowledge into Talmudic and Christian categories and then to hierarchize these categories as abject and rational. Thus, Petrus Alfonsi is able to deny the construction of coevalness with the rabbi even as they speak. Such detemporalization is a key symptom of colonial encounter.

17. For selected works regarding "mappings" among the Victorines, see Anna-Dorthee von den Brincken, "Mappa mundi und Chronographia," *Deutsches Archiv für Erforschung des Mittelalters* 24 (1968): 118–86; "'Imago Mundi' Marginalien zum 'Weltbild' des Honorius Augustodunensis inbes. Imago Mundi I, 1 und 5–7," in *Scientia und Ars im Hoch- und Spätmittelalter*, ed. Ingrid Cramer-Ruegenberg and Adreas Speer, Miscellanea medievalia 22 (Berlin: de Gruyter, 1994), 819–27. Rebecca Moore offers an excellent overview of Hugh of St. Victor studies and an analysis of his exegesis in her monograph, *Jews and Christians in the Life and Thought of Hugh of St. Victor* (Atlanta: Scholars Press, 1998); see also Patrick Gautier Dalché, ed., *La "Descriptio mappe mundi" de Hugues de Saint-Victor* (Paris: Études Augustiniennes, 1988); "Le Renouvellement de la perception et de la représentation de l'espace au XII siècle," in *Renovación intelectual del Occidente europeo siglo XII*, ed. García de Cortázar and José Ángel, Semana de Estudios Medievales 24 (Pamplona: Gobierno de Navarra, 1998), 169–218; Valerie Flint, "World History in the Early Twelfth Century: The *Imago mundi* of Honorius Augustodunensis," in *The Writing of History in the Middle Ages: Essays Presented to Richard William Southern*, ed. R. H. C. Davis and J. M. Wallace-Hadrill (Oxford: Clarendon Press, 1981), 211–38; Flint's edition: "Honorius Augustodunensis: *Imago mundi*," *Archives d'histoire doctrinale et littéraire du moyen âge* 49 (1982): 7–153; and Kupfer, "Medieval World Maps."

18. Roy J. Deferrari, *Hugh of Saint Victor on the Sacraments of the Christian Faith* (Cambridge, Mass.: Medieval Academy of America, 1951), 27.

19. Gautier Dalché, ed., *La "Descriptio mappe mundi"*, 133.

20. Like the Eucharist, which increasingly went on display from the twelfth century to ease anxiety about the absent body of the historical Christ, the *mappaemundi* reminded Christians that they were making "progress." As Richard Southern has remarked, in his essay "Hugh of St. Victor and the Idea of Historical Development," *Transactions of the Royal Historical Society* 21 (1971): 159–71, "the sense of movement [for Hugh of St. Victor] from the primitive to the fully developed state of mankind is quite unlike anything in Augustine or Bede" (167). Michal Kobialka studies the transformation of representation and I would add to his story a cartographic dimension: *This Is My Body: Representational Practices in the Early Middle Ages* (Ann Arbor: University of Michigan Press, 1999). It is therefore not surprising to note the dynamic quality of *mappaemundi* on which refined geographical information garnered from portolan charts and other sources did get mapped. See also Michel de Certeau, "The New Science," in *The Mystic Fable* (Chicago: University of Chicago Press, 1992), 84–85; and Gautier Dalché, ed., *La "Descriptio mappe mundi"*, 94.

21. Beryl Smalley, *The Study of the Bible in the Middle Ages* (Notre Dame, Ind.: University of Notre Dame Press, 1964), 362. Also on the Victorines see Rainer Berndt, "The School of St. Victor in Paris," in *Hebrew Bible/Old Testament: The History of Its Interpretation*, vol. 1, part 2, ed. Magne Saebø (Göttingen: Vandenhoeck and Ruprecht, 2000), 467–96. For a classic study of the impact of Jewish scholars on the Victorines see Herman Hailperin, *Rashi and the Christian Scholars* (Pittsburgh: University of Pittsburgh Press, 1963).

22. For my purposes here, I am interested only in the intertwining of an apocalyptic tradition of Gog and Magog with the identification of Jews as the enclosed peoples of Gog and Magog. See Scott D. Westrem (a participant in the 1995 *Text and Territory* sessions at Kalamazoo), "Against Gog and Magog," in *Text and Territory: Geographical Imagination in the European Middle Ages*, ed. Sylvia Tomasch and Sealy Gilles (Philadelphia: University of Pennsylvania Press, 1998) for other traditions and variations which Gow supplements in his essay on "Gog and Magog," and also in his study, "Kartenrand, Gesellschaftsrand, Geschichtsrand: Die legendären *iudei clausi/inclusi* auf mittelalterlichen und frühneuzeitlichen Weltkarten," *Wolfenbütteler Forschungen* 70 (1996): 137–55. Geraldine Heng helps us to understand some of the traumatic resonance of locating Gog and Magog type monsters back in European imaginary space in her essay, "Cannibalism, the First Crusade, and the Genesis of Medieval Romance," *Differences* 10 (1998): 98–174. Some of the differences in opinion seem to stem from the tensions between image and text in medieval mapping. For more on this problem see, Magriet Hoogvliet, "Mappae Mundi and Medieval Encyclopaedias: Image Versus Text," in *Pre-Modern Encyclopaedic Texts*, ed. Peter Binkley, Brill Studies in Intellectual History 79 (New York: Brill, 1997), 63–75. For the Beatus tradition, see John Williams, *The Illustrated Beatus* (London: Harvey Miller, 1991). Andrew Runni Anderson, *Alexander's Gate, Gog and Magog, and the Legend of the Inclosed Nations* (Cambridge, Mass: Medieval Academy of America, 1932), offers a survey of the complicated medieval tradition of the enclosed peoples of Gog and Magog. See Westrem and Gow for some problems with Anderson.

23. Von den Brincken ("Mappa mundi") gives a useful "check-list" of different loci and motifs and their appearance on *mappaemundi*.

24. See Anderson, *Alexander's Gate*, 63.

25. Gautier Dalché, ed., *La "Descriptio mappe mundi"*, 145.

26. *Historica Scholastica*, quoted in Andrew Anderson, *Alexander's Gate*, 65.

27. Jonathan Goldberg's essay "The History That Will Be," *Gay and Lesbian Quarterly* 1, 4 (1995): 385–404, has guided me here.

28. John Mandeville, *Mandeville's Travels* (MS. Cotton Titus.c XVI), ed. P. Hamelius, Early English Text Society 153 (London: Kegan Paul, 1916), 53.

29. For important studies of the *Travels*, see Mary B. Campbell, *The Witness and the Other World: Exotic European Travel Writing* (Ithaca, N.Y.: Cornell University Press, 1988); Christiane Deluz, *Le Livre de Jehan de Mandeville: une "géographie" au XIVe siècle*, Publications de l'Institut d'Études Médiévales, Textes, Études, Congrès 8 (Louvain: Institut d'Études Médiévales, 1988); Stephen Greenblatt, "From the Dome of the Rock to the Rim of the World," in *Marvelous Possessions: The Wonders of the New World* (Chicago: University of Chicago Press, 1991), 26–51; Iain Macleod Higgins, *Writing East: The "Travels" of Sir John Mandeville* (Philadelphia: University of Pennsylvania Press, 1997); Ralph Hanna, III, "Mandeville," in *Middle English Prose: A Critical Guide to Major Authors and Genres*, ed. A. S. G. Edwards (New Brunswick, N.J.: Rutgers University

Press, 1984), 121–33; and Iain Higgins, "Imagining Christendom from Jerusalem to Paradise: Asia in Mandeville's Travels," in *Discovering New Worlds: Essays on Medieval Exploration and Imagination*, ed. Scott D. Westrem (New York: Garland, 1991), 91–114.

30. Greenblatt, "From the Dome," 50. When I developed my argument for the 1995 Kalamazoo meeting, I was unaware that Benjamin Braude had similar concerns about the elision of Jews in discussions of Mandevillian tolerance. See his "Mandeville's Jews Among Others," in *Pilgrims and Travelers to the Holy Land*, ed. Bryan F. Le Beau and Menachem Mor, Studies in Jewish Civilization 7 (Omaha, Neb.: Creighton University Press, 1996), 133–35.

31. The following works have guided this work on "astrological" theology: T. Gregory, "Temps astrologique et temps chrétien," in *Le Temps chrétien de la fin de l'antiquité au moyen âge, III–XIII siècle*, ed. Jean-Marie Leroux (Paris: Centre National de la Recherche Scientifique, 1984), 557–73; Flint, "World History"; Krzystof Pomian, "Astrology as Natural Theology of History," in *"Astrologi hallucinati": Stars at the End of the World in Luther's Time*, ed. Paolo Zambelli (New York: De Gruyter, 1986), 29–43; Laura Ackerman Smoller, *History, Prophecy and the Stars* (Princeton, N.J.: Princeton University Press, 1994); Bernard McGinn, "Portraying Antichrist in the Middle Ages," in *The Use and Abuse of Eschatology in the Middle Ages*, ed. Werner Verbeke, Daniel Verhelst, and Andries Welkenhuysen, Mediaevalia Lovaniensia ser. 1, Studie 15 (Leuven: Leuven University Press, 1988), 1–49; and J. D. North, "Astrology and the Fortune of Churches," *Centaurus* 24 (1980): 181–211.

32. See Gregory, "Temps astrologique," 566; and also, "L'on comprend comment le temps ponctué par les astres—selon lequel s'articule maintenant le temps de l'histoire des hommes—est quelque chose de différént du temps biblique: tandis que ce dernier est qualifié et défini à partir d'une série d'interventions divines uniques" (560).

33. For instance, see the facsimile with comment in Heinrich Theodor Musper, ed., *Der Antichrist und Die Fünfzehn Zeichen* (Munich: Prestel Verlag, 1970). Popular German *Blochbücher* of the fifteenth century were based on the *Compendium theologicae veritatis* of Hugh Ripelin of Strassburg (d. 1268). He links the ten lost tribes of Israel with the enclosed tribes of Gog and Magog and equates Antichrist with the Jewish Messiah. See also references in n. 22 above, as well as Vincent DiMarco, "The Amazons and the End of the World," in *Discovering New Worlds*, ed. Westrem, 69–90.

34. In 1995, when the early version of this chapter was prepared there existed no comprehensive study of the occurrence of the alphabets in different manuscripts and printed editions of Mandeville. A more recent work can now be noted: Elmar Seebold, "Mandevilles Alphabete und die Mittelalterlichen Alphabetsammlungen," *Beiträge zur Geschichte der deutschen Sprache und Literatur* 20 (1998): 435–99. What interests me for the purposes of my argument is Mandeville's textual allusions to the alphabet in the Hamelius edition from which I cite. Discussion of the alphabets in Mandeville occurs in Josephine Waters Bennett, *The Rediscovery of Sir John Mandeville* (New York: Modern Language Association, 1954), 65–66 and passim; Malcolm Letts, *Sir John Mandeville: The Man and His Book* (London: Batchworth Press, 1949), 151–60; and Deluz, *Le Livre*, 162–73. These alphabets proliferate in manuscripts over time. By around 1390 in Otto von Diemerignen's translation of *Mandeville* into German, additional alphabets are provided for the Chinese and for Prester John, and a Dutch version of the *Travels*, copied in 1430, has

seventeen alphabets (see Bennet, *Rediscovery*, 5). Regarding the related issue of fonts in printed versions, see Alexander Marx, "Some Notes on the Use of Hebrew Type in non-Hebrew Books, 1475–1520," in *Bibliographic Essays: A Tribute to Wilberforce Eames* (Freeport, N.Y.: Books for Libraries Press, 1924), 381–408, who notes that no moveable Hebrew types were used in Christian books of the fifteenth century, in spite of the availability of Hebrew moveable type in Jewish printing houses. Those Hebrew letters that were actually printed were printed off woodblocks in which the entire alphabet was carved.

35. Here is an example of a description of difference defined by astrology:

> For men of ynde han this condicioun of kynde that thei nevere gon out of here owne countree, and therfore is ther gret multitude of peple, but thei ben not sterynge ne mevable, because that thei ben in the firste clymat, that is of Saturne; and Saturne is slough and littill mevynge. For he taryeth to make his turn be the xii. signes xxx. yeer. And the mone passeth thorgh the xii. signes in o moneth. And for because that Saturne is of so late sterynge therefore the folk of that contree that ben under his clymat han of kynde no will for to meve ne stere to seche strange places. And in our contrey is all the contrarie, For wee ben in the seventhe clymate that is of the mone. And the mone is of lyghtly mevynge and the mone is plantete of weye. And for that skyll is it geveth us will of kynde for to meve lyghtly and for to go dyverse weyes and to sechen strange thinges and other dyversitees of the world. For the mone envyronneth the erthe more hastyly than any other planete. (Mandeville, *Travels*, 108)

36. R. Po-chia Hsia, *The Myth of Ritual Murder: Jews and Magic in Reformation Germany* (New Haven, Conn.: Yale University Press, 1988); Gavin Langmuir, *Toward a Definition of Antisemitism* (Berkeley: University of California Press, 1990), 263–82. For a study of Christian representations of cannibalism in travel writings of the thirteenth century, especially the reports on Mongols, see Gregory G. Guzman, "Reports on Mongol Cannibalism in the Thirteenth-Century Latin Sources: Oriental Fact or Western Fiction," in *Discovering New Worlds*, ed. Westrem, 31–67; and Jill Tattersall, "Anthropophagi and Eaters of Raw Flesh in French Literature of the Crusade Period: Myth, Tradition, and Reality," *Medium Aevum* 57 (1988): 240–53. These traditions frequently conflated the enclosed tribes of Gog and Magog with cannibals. Inscriptions on the Hereford *mappaemundi* make this association explicit: "here there are savages who feed on human flesh and drink human blood, accursed sons of Cain. God shut them in through the agency of Alexander the Great; for when an earthquake occurred, the king saw mountains torn from the earth and thrown up as a barrier against them, and where the mountains were lacking, he himself surrounded them with an impassable wall" (quoted in Guzman, "Reports on Mongol Cannibalism," 49).

37. An English astrolabe fabricated in the mid-fourteenth century used the gothic capitals of the alphabet to mark every fifteenth interval of the 360 degrees at the border of the astrolabe (see Gunther, *Astrolabes*, no. 299 for a photograph of the Painswick astrolabe). The alphabet begins, then, to hold important increments on the astrolabe; the alphabet is colonizing the astrolabe itself at the same moment that the narrator of Mandeville oscillated between the astrolabe and the alphabet. Edgar Laird describes the conflation

of alphabet with hourly increments and notes that for the kind of astrolabe described by Chaucer, "the conventions relating degrees to hours, already quite firm, have been literally inscribed [as alphabets] in the astrolabe." See his "Astrolabes and the Construction of Time in the Late Middle Ages," *Disputatio* 2 (1997): 51–69.

38. Mandeville, *Travels*, 120.

39. The medieval epistolary tradition of Prester John tells the story of Gog and Magog, and versions of that story identify the ten lost tribes of Israel as the enclosed people. See Vsevolod Slessarev, *Prester John: The Letter and the Legend* (Minneapolis: University of Minnesota Press, 1959); Alauddin Samarrai, "Beyond Belief and Reverence: Medieval Mythological Ethnography in the Near East and Europe," *Journal of Medieval and Renaissance Studies* 23 (1993): 19–42; Gow, "Gog and Magog." Scholars do not agree on the various stages of emergence of Yiddish. On the question of medieval Christian perceptions that the Jews among whom they lived spoke an "incomprehensible" language, see Yacov Guggenheim, "Meeting on the Road: Encounters Between German Jews and Christians on the Margins of Society," in *In and Out of the Ghetto: Jewish-Gentile Relations in Late Medieval and Early Modern Germany*, ed. R. Po-Chia Hsia and Hartmut Lehmann (New York: Cambridge University Press, 1995), 125–36, especially page 131, where Guggenheim informs us that there are no "unequivocal remains of a distinctly Jewish language in the German lands before 1350." In the same volume Paul Wexler rehearses some of the debates over the origins of Ashkenazic German: "Languages in Contact: The case of *Rotwelsch* and the two 'Yiddishes,'" 109–24. Sander L. Gilman traces the Enlightenment problem with Yiddish as a language to be biologized in his *Jewish Self-Hatred: Anti-Semitism and the Hidden Language of the Jews* (Baltimore: Johns Hopkins University Press, 1986).

40. Mandeville, *Travels*, 177.

41. Mandeville, *Travels*, 178.

42. Greenblatt, "From the Dome," 27.

43. Mandeville, *Travels*, 53.

44. I am drawing on notions of deterritorialization to be found in Gilles Deleuze and Félix Guattari, *Anti-Oedipus: Capitalism and Schizophrenia* (Minneapolis: University of Minnesota Press, 1983).

45. As Chaucer describes:

> in the year of our Lord 1391, on the 12th day of March, I wished to know the time of the day. I took the altitude of my sun, and found that it was 25 degrees and 30 minutes of height in the border on the backside. I then turned my astrolabe, and because it was before midday, I turned my rete and set the degree of the sun; that is to say the 1st degree of Aries, on the right side of my astrolabe, upon that 25 degrees and 30 minutes of height among the almicanteras; then I laid my label upon the degree of my sun, and found the point of my label in the border, upon a capital that is named an X; then I counted all the capital letters from the line of midnight to the aforesaid letter X, and found that it was 9 o'clock of the day. (Gunther, *Chaucer and Messahalla*, 30)

46. When it comes to the Arabic alphabet, the narrator of Mandeville writes: "and iiii lettres thei have more than othere for dbersites of hire langage and speche, for als moche as thei speken in here throtes. And wee in Englond

have in oure langage and speche ii lettres mo than thei have in hire ABD and that is [here follow the characters] the whiche ben clept thorn and zogh" (Mandeville, *Travels*, 92). The implication here is that the Latin alphabet is the exemplary one in comparison to which other alphabets have fewer or more letters.

47. My argument here is based on meditations on mimetic excess in European colonialism; see Michael Taussig, *Mimesis and Alterity: A Particular History of the Senses* (New York: Routledge, 1993).

48. I have consulted the following works on fifteenth-century alphabets: Pierre Dumon, *L'Alphabet gothique dit de Marie de Bourgogne: reproduction du codex Bruxellensis II 845* (Antwerp: Nederlandsche Boekhandel, 1973); M. D. Feld, "Constructed Letters and Illuminated Texts: Regiomontanus, Leon Battista Alberti, and the Origins of Roman Type," *Harvard Library Bulletin* 28 (1980): 357–79; and also his "The First Roman Printers and the Idioms of Humanism," *Harvard Library Bulletin* 36 (1988): 10–91; Damianus Moyllus, *The Moyllus Alphabet: A Newly Discovered Treatise on Classic Letter Design Printed at Parma c. 1480*, ed. Stanley Morrison (New York: Pegasus, 1927).

49. For background on the "return" of Ptolemy's *Geography* to the West and its printing history see the following selected works: Gautier Dalché, "Le Souvenir de la *Géographie*"; John Larner, "The Church and the Quattrocento Renaissance in Geography," *Renaissance Studies* 12 (1989): 26–39; Józef Babicz, "Donnus Nicolaus Germanus—Probleme seiner Biographie und sein Platz der Rezeption der ptolemäischen Geographie," in *Land und Seekarten in Mittelalter und in der frühen Neuzeit*, ed. Cornelis Koeman, Wolfenbütteler Forschungen 7 (Munich: Kraus, 1980), 9–42; Dana Bennett Durand, *The Vienna-Klosterneuburg Map Corpus of the Fifteenth Century* (Leiden: Brill, 1952); Samuel Y. Edgerton, "Florentine Interest in Ptolemaic Cartography as Background for Renaissance Painting, Architecture, and the Discovery of America," *Journal of the Society of Architectural Historians* 33 (1974): 274–92; Deno J. Geanakoplos, "Italian Humanism and the Byzantine Émigré Scholars," in *Renaissance Humanism: Foundations, Forms, Legacy*, vol. 1, *Humanism in Italy*, ed. Albert Rabil (Philadelphia: University of Pennsylvania Press, 1988), 350–81; A. E. Nordenskiöld, *Facsimile Atlas to the Early History of Cartography*, English ed. (1889; reprint New York: Dover, 1973); Robert Weiss, "Jacopo Angeli Da Scarperia (c. 1360–1410–11)," *Medioevo e rinascimento: studi in onore di Bruno Nardi* (Firenze: Sansoni, 1955), 801–27. The return has to be dated from the "wave of Greek studies" ushered in by Manuel Chrysoloras' arrival in Florence in 1397. A letter from Coluccio Salutati (chancellor of Florence, 1375–1410) mentions that Chrysoloras had begun translation of Ptolemy's *Geography* (quoted in Geanakoplos, "Italian Humanism," 354). Jacopo Angeli da Scarperia took up this translation—there is some evidence that he dedicated the translation to Pope Gregory XII (d. 1406) and then to Alexander V, his successor. Nordenskiöld notes a date of 1409–10 for the translation (*Facsimile Atlas*, 10). Nordenskiöld reviews the printed editions of the *Geography* to Paris 1883. See also Joseph Fischer, *Géographie de Ptolémée: traduction latine de Jacopo d'Angiolo de Florence*, BN MS Latin 4802 (Paris: Bibliothèque Nationale, 1926); Henry N. Stevens in his *Ptolemy's Geography: A Brief Account of All the Printed Editions down to 1730* (London: H. Stevens, 1908) reviews the printed editions to 1730. The first printed edition of the *Geography* with a definite date appeared in Vicenza (without maps) in 1475; the date of the Bologna edition (1477) is debated. Then followed a Rome edition in 1478; a metrical version, Florence

1482; Ulm 1482, 1486; Rome 1490, 1507, 1508; Venice 1511; Strassburg 1513, 1520, 1522, 1525. The *Geography* was retranslated and also published with other geographical treatises after 1500; see Stevens, *Ptolemy's Geography* for details. See also William Harris Stahl, *Ptolemy's Geography: A Select Bibliography* (New York: New York Public Library, 1953), for a dated but nevertheless very useful nineteenth-century bibliography.

50. Lisa Jardine, *Erasmus, Man of Letters: The Construction of Charisma in Print* (Princeton, N.J.: Princeton University Press, 1993), 24. I have found Jardine's work on the circulation of the work of Erasmus very helpful for conceptualizing the editions of Ptolemy. She encourages the reader not to view the "edition" as an enclosed, self-contained entity but rather to question how we have arrived at such a modernist fiction of the book: "the book itself is a vital part of the narrative reconstruction of the early modern past. No longer to be seen as a transparent medium, through which the voice of history persists as a trace on the printed page, the book is the physical evidence of assumptions and motives which have to be added to the textual trace of the page to yield a contextualised reading which in turn we make our own" (175).

51. See R. A. Skelton's introduction to the facsimile of Francesco Berlinghieri's work: *Francesco Berlinghieri Geographia: Florence 1482* (Amsterdam: Theatrum Orbis Terrarum, 1966). The Ulm 1482 version does not provide the reader with any editorial tools, such as alphabetized lists of provinces or alphabetized lists of places within each of the regional sections. See Martha Tedeschi, "Publish and Perish: The Career of Lienhart Holle in Ulm," in *Printing the Written Word: The Social History of Books, circa 1450–1520*, ed. Sandra L. Hindman (Ithaca, N.Y.: Cornell University Press, 1991), 41–67; for a facsimile see Skelton, *Claudius Ptolomaeus Cosmographia*.

52. For a very general introduction to typeface by region and genre in the fifteenth century, see Henri-Jean Martin, *The History and Power of Writing*, trans. Lydia G. Cochrane (Chicago: University of Chicago Press, 1994), 303–5.

53. The noted mathematician Regiomantanus used Roman type fonts for printing his scientific works, notably the *Astronomica* of Manlius.

54. The descriptive text for some of the cities, which appears in the *Registrum alphabeticum* of the Ulm 1486 Ptolemy, was translated from a text (Bruxelles: B.R. MS 11.038) dedicated by Jean Germain to Philip the Good, Duke of Burgundy, in 1449. Germain, who was noted for his "Turkish studies" in the Burgundian court, served as chancellor of the Order of the Golden Fleece and as bishop of Chalon-sur-Saone. The intersections of aristocratic courts, astrology, and the alphabet are clear in the criss-crossing traces they left on the 1486 Ptolemy.

55. Berlinghieri relied on sources other than Ptolemy for his version of *Ptolemy's Geography*, but these borrowings occur within the treatise itself and not as added matter at the front or back.

56. The Strassburg Ptolemy is the first to separate the "classic" Ptolemaic maps in a distinct section "intact and separate in its ancient form" as the editors wrote, from modern maps, or in their words: "a representation of the three parts of the world more proper to our time." For a facsimile, see Skelton, *Claudius Ptolomaeus Cosmographia*.

57. This mini-encyclopedia, composed primarily of excerpts from Isidore, traveled with subsequent editions of Ptolemy's *Geography* to the Strassburg 1513 edition.

58. For references to alphabetization, an editorial tool at least three

centuries old by the time of this Ptolemy edition, see the following: Lloyd W. Daly, *Contributions to a History of Alphabetization in Antiquity and the Middle Ages*, Collection Latomus 90 (Bruxelles: Berchem, 1968); Ivan Illich, *In the Vineyard of the Text: A Commentary to Hugh's* Didascalicon (Chicago: University of Chicago Press, 1993); Ivan Illich and Barry Sanders, *ABC: The Alphabetization of the Popular Mind* (New York: Vintage, 1988); and Karin Miethaner-Vent, "Das Alphabet in der mittelalterlichen Lexikographie: Verwendungsweisen, Formen und Entwicklung des alphabetischen Anordnungsprinzips," in *La Lexicographie au moyen âge*, ed. C. Buridant (Lille: Presses Universitaires, 1986), 83–112.

59. For general discussions of Renaissance Christian-Hebrew studies, see Robert Bonfil, *Jewish Life in Renaissance Italy* (Berkeley: University of California Press, 1994), 145–78; Hsia, *The Myth of Ritual Murder*; Daniel B. Ruderman, "The Italian Renaissance and Jewish Thought," in *Renaissance Humanism*, ed. Rabil, 382–483. For an excellent discussion of Manetti, see Christoph Dröge, "'Quia Morem Hieronymi in Transferendo Cognovi. . . .' Les débuts des études hébraïques chez les humanistes italien," in *L'Hébreu au temps de la Renaissance*, ed. Ilana Zinguer (New York: Brill, 1992), 65–88; and for Pico, see Chaim Wirszubski, *Pico della Mirandola's Encounter with Jewish Mysticism* (Cambridge, Mass.: Harvard University Press, 1989).

60. Here is it important to note that Pico relied on the translations of Flavius Mithridates, a Jewish convert, for his study of Kabbala. On Good Friday 1481, Mithridates preached a sermon to the popes and cardinals in the Vatican in which he presented "secret Jewish evidences from a pre-Christian 'old Talmud' confirming the mysteries of Christ's Passion" (quoted in Wirszubski, *Pico della Mirandola's Encounter*, 106). See also Jerome Friedman, "The Myth of Jewish Antiquity: New Christians and Christian Hebraica in Early Modern Europe," in *Jewish Christian and Christian Jews: From the Renaissance to the Enlightenment*, ed. Richard H. Popkin and Gordon M. Weiner (Boston, Mass.: Kluwer Academic, 1994), 35–56; and Bernard McGinn, "Cabalists and Christians: Reflections on Cabala in Medieval and Renaissance Thought," 11–34.

61. The "technological" means of arriving at this body of the "classic" (pre-supersessionary) Jew involved procedures through which the Hebrew language was converted into a number code. In his important study of Pico and Kabbala, Wirszubski has shown how the translations of Mithridates interpolated these "ciphering" practices during translation. Elsewhere Hsia has called Christian-Hebrew studies the "disenchantment" of Hebrew. According to Wirszubski, this disenchantment paradoxically involved its technologization through philology and natural magic: "Pico viewed Kabbala from an entirely new standpoint: he is the first Christian who considered Kabbala to be simultaneously a witness for Christianity and an ally of natural magic" (151).

62. For fuller discussion of this trial and engravings and the problem of inscription in Christian-Jewish ethnic conflict, see the next chapter, and R. Po-Chia Hsia, *Trent 1475: Stories of a Ritual Murder Trial* (New Haven, Conn.: Yale University Press, 1992); and Hsia's *The Myth of Ritual Murder*.

63. The work of Miri Rubin has untangled the relations of the cult of the Eucharist to the status of medieval Jews, *Gentile Tales: The Narrative Assault on Late Medieval Jews* (New Haven, Conn.: Yale University Press, 1999). See also my article "Genders, Bodies, Borders: Technologies of the Visible," *Speculum* 68 (1993): 389–418.

64. Nordenskiöld, *Facsimile Atlas*, 64. Since the presentation of an early

version of this essay in 1995, Gow has offered an exhaustive catalog of such instances in his essay, "Gog and Magog on Mappaemundi and Early Printed World Maps."

65. Walter D. Mignolo, "Signs and Their Transmission: The Question of the Book in the New World," in *Writing Without Words: Alternative Literacies in Mesoamerica and the Andes*, ed. Elizabeth Hill Boone and Walter D. Mignolo (Durham, N.C.: Duke University Press, 1994), 220–70; and Mignolo's *Darker Side of the Renaissance: Literacy, Territoriality, and Colonization* (Ann Arbor: University of Michigan Press, 1995); also thought-provoking is Vicente Rafael, *Contracting Colonialism: Translation and Christian Conversion in Tagalog Society Under Early Spanish Rule* (Durham, N.C.: Duke University Press, 1993).

66. Evelyn Fox Keller, "From Secrets of Life to Secrets of Death," in *Body/Politics: Women and the Discourses of Science*, ed. Mary Jacobus, Evelyn Fox Keller, and Sally Shuttleworth (New York: Routledge, 1990), 177–91; and Stephen S. Hall, *Mapping the Next Millennium: How Computer-Driven Cartography Is Revolutionizing the Face of Science* (New York: Vintage, 1993); Lily E. Kay, *Who Wrote the Book of Life? A History of the Genetic Code* (Stanford, Calif.: Stanford University Press, 2000).

Chapter 2. Printing Excision: The Graphic Afterlife of Medieval Universal Histories

An earlier version of this essay, "Becoming Collection: The Spatial Afterlife of Medieval Universal Histories," appeared in *Medieval Spatial Practices*, ed. Barbara A. Hanawalt and Michal Kobialka (Minneapolis: University of Minnesota Press, 2000), 223–41.

1. Adrian Wilson, *The Making of the Nuremberg Chronicle* (Amsterdam: Nico Israel, 1976), 52. Maximilian I held his Reichstag in Nuremberg in 1491 and resided there for six months. His imperial presence undoubtedly inspired the grandiose *Chronicle* project. See also Christoph Reske, *Die Produktion der Schedelschen Weltchronik*, Mainzer Studien zür Buchwissenschaft 10 (Wiesbaden: Harrassowitz Verlag, 2000) and his essay, "The Printer Anton Koberger and his Printing Shop," *Gutenberg-Jahrbuch* 76 (2001): 98–103.

2. James Samuel Preus analyzes this important shift in the Christian typological imaginary in his *From Shadow to Promise: Old Testament Interpretation from Augustine to Young Luther* (Cambridge, Mass.: Harvard University Press, 1969). This chapter locates its analysis discursively between Preus and two other trenchant analyses of transformation in representation, which are relevant, I argue, to the typological imaginary: Ann Kibbey, *The Interpretation of Material Shapes in Puritanism: A Study of Rhetoric, Prejudice, and Violence* (New York: Cambridge University Press, 1986); Thomas H. Luxon, *Literal Figures: Puritan Allegory and the Reformation Crisis in Representation* (Chicago: University of Chicago Press, 1995).

3. Karl Heinrich Krüger provides an overview and introductory bibliography in his study, *Die Universalchroniken* (Turnout: Brepols, 1976). For a nuanced contrast of universal history with prose chronicles, see Gabrielle M. Spiegel, "Genealogy: Form and Function in Medieval Historical Narrative," *History and Theory* 22 (1983): 43–53. See also these indispensable introductions: Anna-Dorothee von den Brincken, "Mappa mundi und Chronographia: Studien zur imago mundi des abendländischen Mittelalters," *Deutsches Archive*

für Erforschung des Mittelalters 24 (1968): 118–86; and her "Die lateinische Weltchronistik," in *Mensch und Weltgeschichte: Zur Geschichte der Universalsgeschichtsschreibung*, ed. Alexander Randa, Internationales Forschungszentrum für Grundfragen der Wissenschaften Salzburg (Salzburg: Anton Pustet, 1969), 43–86; Hans-Werner Goetz, "On the Universality of Universal History," in *L'Historiographie médiévale en Europe*, ed. Jean-Phillipe Genet (Paris: Centre National de la Recherche Scientifique, 1991), 247–62.

4. The graphic design of universal history has been discussed by Gert Melville, "Geschichte in graphischer Gestalt. Beobachtungen zu einer spätmittelalterlichen Darstellungsweise," in *Geschichtsschreibung und Geschichtsbewußtsein im späten Mittelalter*, ed. Hans Patze, Vorträge und Forschungen 31 (Sigmaringen: Jan Thorbecke, 1987), 57–156.

5. For a general introduction to *mappaemundi*, see discussion and notes in Chapter 1. For a recent survey of *mappaemundi* that have Jerusalem inscribed as the center of the world, see Iain Macleod Higgins, "Defining the Earth's Center in a Medieval 'Multi-Text': Jerusalem in *The Book of John Mandeville*," in *Text and Territory: Geographical Imagination in the European Middle Ages*, ed. Sylvia Tomasch and Sealy Gilles (Philadelphia: University of Pennsylvania Press, 1998), 29–53; and Kerstin Hengevoss-Dürkop, "Jerusalem—Das Zentrum der Ebstorf-Karte," in *Ein Weltbild vor Columbus: Die Ebstorfer Weltkarte. Interdisziplinäres Colloquium*, ed. Hartmut Kugler and Eckhard Michael (Weinheim: VCH, 1991). For other discussions of representation of cities on *mappaemundi*, see Hartmut Kugler, *Die Vorstellung der Stadt in der Literatur des deutschen Mittelalters* (München: Artemis Verlag, 1986); Bianca Kühnel, *From the Earthly to the Heavenly Jerusalem: Representations of the Holy City in Christian Art of the First Millennium*, Römische Quartalschrift für Christliche Altertumskunde und Kirchengeschichte, Supplementheft 42 (Freiburg: Herder, 1987); Daniel Poiron, ed., *Jerusalem, Rome, Constantinople: l'image et le mythe de la ville*, Cultures et Civilisations Médiévales 5 (Paris: Presses de l'Université de Paris-Sorbonne, 1986); and Franz Niehoff, "Umbilicus Mundi: Der Nabel der Welt," in *Ornamenta Ecclesiae: Kunst and Künstler der Romanik*, ed. Anton Legner (Cologne: Schnütgen-Museum, 1985), 53–72.

6. See Anna-Dorothee von den Brincken, "Die Rezeption mittelalterlicher Historiographie durch den Inkunabeldruck," in *Geschichtsschreibung und Geschichtsbewußtsein*, 215–37.

7. Margaret Bingham Stillwell, "The Fasciculus Temporum: A Genealogical Survey of Editions Before 1480," in *Bibliographic Essays: A Tribute to Wilberforce Eames* (Freeport, N.Y.: Books for Libraries, 1924), 409–40.

8. Melville, "Geschichte in graphische Gestalt," 82.

9. For both the *Supplementum chronicarum* and the *Fasciculus*, city views were simply added to an already existent text; see Achim Krümmel, *Das "Supplementum Chronicarum" des Augustinermönches Jacobus Phillipus Foresti von Bergamo*, Bibliothemata 6 (Herzverg: Bautz, 1992). Furthermore Krümmel, who has undertaken an exhaustive study of the *Supplementum Chronicarum*, doubts that Foresti von Bergamo had input into the choice and placing of the illustrations for the 1486 edition (151).

10. See V. von Loga, "Die Stadtansichten in Hartmann Schedels Weltchronik," *Jahrbuch der königlich preussischen Kunstsammlungen* 9 (1988): 93–107; 184–96; and Elizabeth Rücker, *Hartmann Schedels Weltchronik* (Munich: Prestel, 1988). For specific analysis of local detail the "realistic" city views of the Nuremberg Chronicle depict and also leave out see the useful study, *Imago*

Civitatis: Stadtbildsprache des Spätmittelalters, ed. Werner Kreuer, Essener Geographische Schriften 2 (Essen: Institut für Geographie, 1993).

11. Severin Corsten, "Der frühe Buchdruck und die Stadt," in *Studien zum städtischen Bildungswesen des späten Mittelalters und der frühen Neuzeit,* ed. Bernd Moeller, Hans Patze, and Karl Stackmann (Göttingen: Vandenhoeck and Ruprecht, 1983), 9–32.

12. This view appears on 99v and 100r.

13. Karl IV ordered leveling of the synagogue to make way for the market on November 16, 1349, at a time when the area would be suffering from the Black Death. See Gerhard Pfeiffer, ed., *Nürnberg—Geschichte einer europäischen Stadt* (Munich: Verlag Beck, 1971), 89–90, 107–8. Jews were expelled from Nuremberg in December 1349, according to Haverkamp, who gives an overview of expulsions and massacres in German cities at the time of the Black Death, Alfred Haverkamp, "Die Judenverfolgungen zur Zeit des Schwarzen Todes in Gesellschaftsgefüge deutscher Städte," in his *Zur Geschichte der Juden im Deutschland des späten Mittelalters und der frühen Neuzeit* (Stuttgart: Hiersemann, 1981), 27–93.

14. The Latin edition of 1493 significantly leaves three pages blank (folios cclviii, cclx, cclxi) between the sixth age and the seventh age of the Last Days in the Latin edition of 1493.

15. "Sie haben diese kirchen mite lere, mit winderzaichen, mit even pilder und mit plutvergissen geplantzt" (fol 101r, facsimile-German edition 1493).

16. Here it is interesting to note the resemblance drawn between Pentecost and printing in the next century by John Foxe in his *Acts and Monuments* (1583 last edition of Foxe): "Notwithstanding, what man soever was the instrument, without all doubt God himself was the ordainer and disposer thereof; no otherwise than he was the gift of tongues, and that for a singular purpose. And well may this gift of printing be resembled to the gift of tongues: for like as God then spake with many tongues, and yet all that would not turn the Jews; so now, when the Holy Ghost speaketh to the adversaries in innumerable sorts of books, yet they will not be converted or turn to the Gospel." This text is cited in Anthony Kemp, *The Estrangement of the Past: A Study in the Origins of Modern Historical Consciousness* (New York: Oxford University Press, 1991), 103.

17. See Kemp, *Estrangement of the Past*; and Richard Kenneth Emmerson, *Antichrist in the Middle Ages: A Study of Medieval Apocalypticism, Art, and Literature* (Seattle: University of Washington Press, 1981), 236.

18. See François Robin, "Jérusalem dans la peinture franco-flamande (XII–XVième siècles): abstractions, fantasies et réalités," in *Jerusalem, Rome, Constantinople,* ed. Poirion, 33–64.

19. See Hans Belting, *Likeness and Presence: A History of the Image Before the Era of Art,* trans. Edmund Jephcott (Chicago: University of Chicago Press, 1994), esp. 470–78. I am joining this critique of Belting to the work of Julia Lupton, *Afterlives of the Saints: Hagiography, Typology, and Renaissance Literature* (Stanford, Calif.: Stanford University Press, 1996).

20. See Christopher S. Wood, *Albrecht Altdorfer and the Origins of Landscape* (London: Reaktion, 1993), for meditations on these traces of voided theological subject matter in the landscapes of Albrecht Altdorfer. More on Altdorfer follows in chapter 3.

21. A translation of the Latin text, which appeared on the advertising flyer for the *Nuremberg Chronicle,* is given in Wilson, *The Nuremberg Chronicle,* 209.

22. Michel de Certeau would call the work of cutting out and the act of

displacing Jerusalem a "strategy": "the calculus of force-relationships which becomes possible when a subject of will and power (a proprietor, an enterprise, a city, a scientific institution) can be isolated from an 'environment.'" *The Practice of Everyday Life*, trans. Steven Rendall (Berkeley: University of California Press, 1988), xix.

23. Albrecht Dürer is alleged to have worked in the workshop of Michael Wolgemut during the time in which the latter was involved with designing the woodcuts for the *Nuremberg Chronicle.* Scholars continue to disagree over his involvement. See Peter Zahn, *Neue Funde zur Entehung der Schedelschen Weltchronik 1493*, Renaissance-Vorträge 213 (Nürnberg: Museen der Stadt, 1973), 193–206, and Reske, *Produktion*, passim. For a study of this self-portrait, see Joseph Lee Koerner, *The Moment of Self-Portraiture in German Renaissance Art* (Chicago: University of Chicago Press, 1993); for another example of such self-allegorization, see Lisa Jardine's study of Erasmus's calculated efforts to stage himself as the "figure of trans-European learning," *Erasmus, Man of Letters: The Construction of Charisma in Print* (Princeton, N.J.: Princeton University Press, 1993), 147.

24. On the spines of his notebooks Schedel would inscribe the motto taken from John 6:12: "Collect the fragments lest they perish" ("Colligite fragmenta ne pereat") (cited in von Loga, "Die Stadtansichten," 102).

25. Jean-Joseph Goux had drawn our attention to the importance of such acts of substitution for both signifying and economic processes in his *Symbolic Economies: After Marx and Freud* (Ithaca, N.Y.: Cornell University Press, 1990), 4.

26. Lupton, *Afterlives of the Saints*, xxix.

27. Richard Stauber, *Die Schedelsche Bibliothek* (Nieuwkoop: De Graaf, 1969).

28. Ingrid D. Rowland, "Revenge of the Regensburg Humanists," *Sixteenth Century Journal* 25 (1994): 307–22.

29. For an overview of the "translation" of Italian humanism in German cities, see Lewis W. Spitz, "The Course of German Humanism," in *Itinerarium Italicum: The Profile of the Italian Renaissance in the Mirror of Its European Transformations*, ed. Heiko Oberman with Thomas A. Brady, Studies in Medieval and Reformation Thought 14 (Leiden: Brill, 1975), 371–435. Conrad Celtis's panegyric to Nuremberg, *Norimbergae* (1495), can be read in a facsimile edition edited by Albert Werminghoff, *Conrad Celtis und sein Buch über Nürnberg* (Freiburg, 1921).

30. See Chapter 1. Luxon writes about ancient Israel as the knot between the slippage of allegory and typology in Puritan "reading" practices. For deteriorating conditions for Jews in Germany and environs in the fifteenth century see Dean Phillip Bell, *Sacred Communities: Jewish and Christian Identities in Fifteenth-Century Germany* (Boston: Brill, 2001); Heiko A. Oberman, "Discovery of Hebrew and Discrimination Against the Jews: The Veritas Hebraica as Double-Edged Sword in Renaissance and Reformation," in *Germania Illustrata*, ed. Andrew C. Fix and Susan C. Karant-Nunn, Sixteenth Century Essays and Studies 18 (Ann Arbor, Mich.: Edwards Brothers, 1992), 19–34; Alexander Patschovsky, "Der 'Talmudjude': Vom mittelalterlichen Ursprung eines neuzeitlichen Themas," *Zeitschrift für Historische Forschung* 13 (1992): 13–28; Charles Zika, "Hosts, Processions and Pilgrimages: Controlling the Sacred in Fifteenth-Century Germany," *Past and Present* 118 (February 1988): 25–64; and R. Po-chia Hsia, *The Myth of Ritual Murder: Jews and Magic in Reformation Germany* (New Haven, Conn.: Yale University Press, 1988); and his "The Usurious

Jew: Economic Structure and Religious Representations in an Anti-Semitic Discourse," in *In and Out of the Ghetto: Jewish-Gentile Relations in Late Medieval and Early Modern Germany*, ed. R. Po-Chia Hsia and Hartmut Lehmann (New York: Cambridge University Press, 1995), 161–76. For specific Christian initiatives against Jews in their last decade in Nuremberg, see Arye Maimon and Yacov Guggenheim, eds., *Germania Judaica*, vol. 3/2, *1350–1519* (Tübingen: J.C.B. Mohr, 1995), 1001–44; Michael Toch, "'Umb Gemeyns Nutz und Nottdurfft Willen': Obrigkeitliches und jurisdiktionelles Denken bei der Austreibung der Nürnberger Juden 1498/99," *Zeitschrift für Historische Forschung* 11 (1984): 1–21; and Arnd Müller, *Geschichte der Juden in Nürnberg: 1146–1945* (Nürnberg: Stadtbibliothek, 1968).

31. Preus, *From Shadow to Promise*, offers an insightful discussion of the importance of "simul" as a temporal category for Luther (209). Its implications for representations of the Apocalypse, especially in Dürer, requires further work.

32. Werminghoff, *Conrad Celtis und sein Buch über Nürnberg*, 199 (Nullam Germaniae urbem immunem reliquere, quam hoc scelere non polluissent, sacris etiam hostiis et sacramentis nostris saepe ablatis contumeliaque et ignominia affectis).

33. See Toch, "'Umb Gemeyns Nutz und Nottdurfft Willen'"; and Maimon and Guggenheim, *Germania Judaica*, for the strategies of the town council to expel Jews beginning in the 1470s. For background on Hans Folz see David Price, "Hans Folz's Anti-Jewish Carnival Plays," *Fifteenth Century Studies* 19 (1992): 209–28; Aaron E. Wright, "'Die gotlich sterk gab daz der teuschen zungen': Folz, Schedel, and the Printing Press in Fifteenth-Century Nuremberg," *Fifteenth Century Studies* 19 (1992): 319–49; Edith Wenzel, "Zur Judenproblematik bei Hanz Folz," *Zeitschrift für Deutsche Philologie* 101 (1982): 79–194; and her "Synagoga und Ecclesia: Zum antijudaismus im deutschsprachigen Spiel des Mittelalters," *Internationale Archive für Sozialgeschichte der deutschen Literatur* 12 (1987): 57–81; Hans Walther, "Hans Folz: Altes und Neues zur Geschichte seines Lebens und seiner Schriften," *Zeitschrift für Deutsches Altertum und Deutsche Literatur* 29 (1966): 212–42.

34. See Wilson, *The Making of the Nuremberg Chronicle*, 176; and Béatrice Hernad, *Die Graphiksammlung des Humanisten Hartmann Schedel* (Munich: Prestel, 1990), 66; for a reflection on the Altdorfer etchings, see Chapter 3.

35. Kibbey, *The Interpretation of Material Shapes in Puritanism*, extends this discussion to the New World and traces how Protestant notions of icons worked to produce the decision to annihilate the Pequots in New England in 1637.

36. See Svetlana Alpers, "The Mapping Impulse in Dutch Art," in *Art and Cartography: Six Historical Essays*, ed. David Woodward (Chicago: University of Chicago Press, 1987), 51–96; Thomas Frangenberg, "Chorographies of Florence: The Use of City Views and City Plans in the Sixteenth Century," *Imago Mundi* 46 (1994): 41–64; Jürgen Schulz, "Jacop de'Barbari's View of Venice: Map Making, City Views, and Moralized Geography Before the Year 1500," *Art Bulletin* 60 (1978): 425–74.

37. The descriptions and views could also be marketed separately without the edifying frontispiece and didactic address to the reader written by one of the editors, Georg Braun. See R. A. Skelton's introduction to the facsimile, *Braun and Hogenberg: Civitates Orbis Terrarum* (New York: World, 1966).

38. Paula Findlen underscores how such collections in the early modern

museum did the work of bringing together "pieces of a cosmology that had all but fallen apart in the course of several centuries." Further she writes: "organizing all known ideas and artifacts under the rubric of museum, collectors imagined that they had indeed come to terms with the crisis of knowledge that the fabrication of the museum was designed to solve." Paula Findlen, *Possessing Nature: Museums, Collecting, and Scientific Culture in Early Modern Italy* (Berkeley: University of California Press, 1994), 50. Krzysztof Pomian, *Collectors and Curiosities: Paris and Venice, 1500–1800* (London: Polity, 1990) views the early-modern collection as a "replacement" (38) of medieval treasure houses and relic collections. See also Anthony Lane Shelton, "Cabinets of Transgression: Renaissance Collections and the Incorporation of the New World," in *The Cultures of Collecting*, ed. John Elsner and Roger Cardinal (Cambridge, Mass.: Harvard University Press, 1994), 177–203.

39. Lupton, *Afterlives of the Saints*, xxi.
40. Lupton, *Afterlives of the Saints*, xxviii.
41. Lupton, *Afterlives of the Saints*, xxviii.

Chapter 3. Graphic Reoccupation, the Faithful Synagogue, Foucault's Genealogy

1. The city view of Regensburg appears on pages 97v and 98r of the German edition of the *Nuremberg Chronicle* (Nuremberg, 1493). See Chapter 2 for further references to the publication of the *Chronicle*. The results of excavation in the medieval Jewish quarter of Regensburg may be found in the following studies: Dean Phillip Bell, *Sacred Communities: Jewish and Christian Identities in Fifteenth-Century Germany* (Boston: Brill, 2001), 12–35; Silvia Codreanu-Windauer and Heinrich Wanderwitz, "Das Regensburger Judenviertel: Geschichte und Archäologie," in *Geschichte der Stadt Regensburg*, vol. 1, ed. Peter Schmid (Regensburg: F. Pustet, 2000), 607–33; Herbert E. Brekle, *Das Regensburger Ghetto* (Regensburg: Mittelbayerische Druck- und Verlags-Gesellschaft, 1997); and Siegfried Wittmer, *Jüdisches Leben in Regensburg von frühen Mittelalter bis 1519* (Regensburg: Universitätsverlag, 2001). My grappling with Altdorfer is inspired by Christopher S. Wood, *Albrecht Altdorfer and the Origins of Landscape* (London: Reaktion, 1993). On the emergence of the aesthetic as an ideological space in the early sixteenth century see Joseph Lee Koerner, *The Moment of Self-Portraiture in German Renaissance Art* (Chicago: University of Chicago Press, 1993). The citation of Dürer may be found as follows: *Schriftlicher Nachlaß*, vol. 2, ed. Hans Rupprich (Berlin: Deutsche Verein fur Kunstwissenschaft), 100; and in translation in *The Writings of Albrecht Dürer*, trans. and ed. William Martin Conway (New York: Philosophical Library), 180.

2. I rely again on the analysis of tranformations in typological thinking in Luther's first lectures on the Psalms (1513–15) by James Samuel Preus, *From Shadow to Promise: Old Testament Interpretation from Augustine to Young Luther* (Cambridge, Mass.: Harvard University Press, 1969). I link Preus's suggestive analysis to the concept of reoccupation developed by Hans Blumenberg, *The Legitimacy of the Modern Age*, trans. Robert M. Wallace (Cambridge, Mass.: MIT Press, 1983). This chapter also shows the need to think of Blumenberg's work through the typological imaginary.

3. Michel de Certeau, "The New Science" in his *The Mystic Fable*, trans. Michael B. Smith (Chicago: University of Chicago Press, 1992), 81.

4. Full references to the polemics discussed here can be found in Chapter 1, note 11; also Alexander Patschovsky, "Der 'Talmudjude': Vom mittelalterlichen Ursprung eines neuzeitlichen Themas," *Zeitschrift für Historische Forschung* 13 (1992): 13–28.

5. On ordeal and inquest, and here only a starting point, see Howard Bloch, *Medieval French Literature and Law* (Berkeley: University of California Press, 1977); Paul R. Hyams, "Trial by Ordeal: The Key to Proof in the Early Common Law," in *On the Laws and Customs of England: Essays in Honor of Samuel E. Thorne*, ed. Morris S. Arnold (Chapel Hill: University of North Carolina Press, 1981), 90–126; Robert Bartlett, *Trial by Fire and Water: The Medieval Judicial Ordeal* (Oxford: Clarendon, 1986); Talal Asad, "Pain and Truth in Medieval Christian Ritual," in *Genealogies of Religion: Discipline and Reasons of Power in Christianity and Islam* (Baltimore: Johns Hopkins University Press, 1993), 83–124; John W. Baldwin, "The Crisis of the Ordeal: Literature, Law, and Religion Around 1200," *Journal of Medieval and Renaissance Studies* 24 (1994), 327–53; Stephen D. White, "Proposing the Ordeal and Avoiding It: Strategy and Power in Western French Litigation, 1050–1110," in *Cultures of Power: Lordship, Status, and Process in Twelfth-Century Europe*, ed. Thomas N. Bisson (Philadelphia: University of Pennsylvania Press, 1995), 89–123. The research of Winfried Trusen shows the importance of studying oaths, ordeals, and inquests as an intertextual problem. See her essay: "Der Inquisitionsprozeß: Seine historische Grundlagen und frühen Formen," *Zeitschrift der Savigny-Stiftung für Rechtsgeschichte, Kanonistische Abteilung* 74 (1988): 168–230. Professor Trusen's thesis that the process of inquiry placed "information" between the accused and the judge, thus displacing the body of the accused, accords well with the thesis developed in this chapter. Suggestive too for problems of inquisitorial writing space and montage: Michel Foucault, *Discipline and Punish: The Birth of the Prison*, trans. Alan Sheridan (New York: Vintage Books, 1979); Gilles Deleuze, *Cinema 2: The Time Image*, trans. Hugh Tomlinson and Robert Galeta (Minneapolis: University of Minnesota Press, 1989); Monique David-Ménard, *Hysteria from Freud to Lacan: Body and Language of Psychoanalysis*, trans. Catherine Porter (Ithaca, N.Y.: Cornell University Press, 1989); Jonathan Goldberg, "The History That Will Be," *Gay and Lesbian Quarterly* 1 (1995): 385–404; and Cathy Caruth, *Unclaimed Experience: Trauma, Narrative, and History* (Baltimore: Johns Hopkins University Press, 1996).

6. Bernhard Blumenkranz, *Disputatio Iudei et Christiani Gilberti Crispini* (Antwerp: Spectrum, 1956), 42.

7. I am drawing on the following discussions of circumcision: Daniel Boyarin, *A Radical Jew: Paul and the Politics of Identity* (Berkeley: University of California Press, 1994); Julia Reinhard Lupton, "*Ethnos* and Circumcision in the Pauline Tradition: A Psychoanalytic Exegesis," in *The Psychoanalysis of Race*, ed. Christopher Lane (New York: Columbia University Press, 1998), 193–210; Julia Reinhard Lupton and Bonita Rhoads, "Circumcising the Antichrist: An Ethno-Historical Fantasy," *Jouvert* 3 (1999)<http://social.chass.ncsu.edu/jouvert/v3i12/rhoad.html>; Leo Steinberg, *The Sexuality of Christ in Renaissance Art and in Modern Oblivion* (Chicago: University of Chicago Press, 1996); Gil Anidjar, "On the (Under)Cutting Edge: Does Jewish Memory Need Sharpening?" in *Jews and Other Differences: The New Jewish Cultural Studies*, ed. Jonathan Boyarin and Daniel Boyarin (Minneapolis: University of Minnesota Press, 1997); Timothy W. Berkley, *From a Broken Covenant to Circumcision of the Heart* (Atlanta: Society of Biblical Literature, 2000).

8. Bruno Latour, "Drawing Things Together," in *Representation in Scientific Practice*, ed. Michael Lynch and Steve Woolgar (Cambridge,Mass.: MIT Press, 1990).

9. For a more detailed explication of the Alfonsi *Dialogi* and subsequent layering of inscriptions in medieval *mappaemundi*, travel literature, and Ptolemaic maps see Chapter 1. Alfonsi's polemic is important for its talmudic references, which introduced knowledge of post-biblical Judaism into the polemical tradition. See Jeremy Cohen, *Living Letters*.

10. Alfonsi's *Dialogi* continued to be copied through the fifteenth century (21 copies in the twelfth century; 24 copies in the thirteenth; 14 copies in the fourteenth; 18 copies in the fifteenth). In only two instances were the Alfonsi and Crispin polemics bound together.

11. For the Latin text and translation, see canon 8 (De inquisitionibus— On Inquests) and canon 18 (De iudicio sanguinis et duelli clericis interdicto—On Sentences Involving Either the Shedding of Blood or a Duel Being Forbidden to Clerics), in Norman P. Tanner, *Decrees of the Ecumenical Councils* (Washington, D.C.: Georgetown University Press,1990), 236–39, 244.

12. The Baruch trial can be found in Jean Duvernoy, ed., *Le Registre d'inquisition de Jacques Fournier (1318–1325)* (New York: Mouton, 1978); for the Trent trial, see Anna Esposito and Diego Quaglioni, *Processi contro gli Ebrei di Trento (1475–1478)* (Padua: CEDAM, 1990); and R. Po-Chia Hsia, *Trent, 1475: Stories of a Ritual Murder Trial* (New Haven, Conn.: Yale University Press, 1992).

13. I am relying on Eric L. Santner's discussion of pleasure and the binding "normative" role of fantasy in his *On the Psychotheology of Everyday Life* (Chicago: University of Chicago Press, 2001), 33. Also crucial to the question of pleasure/knowledge/violence, see Louise O. Fradenburg and Carla Freccero, "The Pleasures of History," *Gay and Lesbian Quarterly* 1 (1995), 373–84. For the importance of the gender and sexuality of inquisitorial inscription, see Kathleen Biddick, "The Devil's Anal Eye: Inquisitorial Optics and Ethnographic Authority," in *The Shock of Medievalism* (Durham, N.C.: Duke University Press, 1998), 105–34.

14. David-Ménard, *Hysteria from Freud to Lacan*, 183.

15. A very important question has not yet been asked and cannot be dealt with adequately here. How did Jews engage in these inscriptional contests? At this juncture the complex story of Hebrew printing in Europe needs to be considered. In brief, 1475, the year of the Trent trial, coincided with the first publication of Hebrew incunabula in Pieve, in the shadow of Padua, less than one hundred miles from Trent, as well as the first printing of Hebrew script in non-Hebrew texts in Germany. In the last quarter of the fifteenth century Hebrew printers could be found in the smaller provincial cities of Mantua, Ferrara, Bologna, Soncino (near Milan), Naples, and Brescia. Noted Hebrew printers such as Gerson Soncino also printed Latin and vernacular texts. Venice came to be the major site of Hebrew printing under David Bomberg, a Christian publisher from Antwerp who worked with Jewish scholars in his printing house. Such collaborations were always vulnerable, and the Venetian republic exacted a high cost. Bomberg had to pay extortionate fees to extend his permission to print Hebrew texts, and the ambivalent attitude to Hebrew publishing flared in 1553, when a papal order condemned printed Talmuds to burning. As a starting point, consult Paul F. Grendler, *The Roman Inquisition and the Venetian Press 1540–1605* (Princeton, N.J.: Princeton University Press, 1977); and David Werner Amram, *The Makers of Hebrew Books in Italy* (London: Holland Press, 1973).

16. Michel Foucault, "Nietzsche, Genealogy, History," in *Language, Counter-Memory, Practice*, trans. Donald Bouchard (Ithaca,N.Y.: Cornell University Press, 1977), 160.

17. Foucault, "Nietzsche, Genealogy, History," 152.

18. Foucault, "Nietzsche, Genealogy, History," 158.

19. Foucault, "Nietzsche, Genealogy, History," 154.

20. Michel Foucault, *History of Sexuality*, vol. 1, *An Introduction*, trans. Robert Hurley (New York: Vintage Books, 1980), 124. From the 1974 French edition: "N'imaginons pas la bourgeoisie se châtrant symboliquement pour mieux refuser aux autres le droit d'avoir un sexe et d'en user à leur gré. . . . Le 'sang' de la bourgeoisie, ce fut son sexe" (164). Foucault himself grappled with these contradictions in his genealogical method, and I believe that they can account in part for the surprising aesthetic unities encountered in volumes 2 and 3 of *The History of Sexuality*. This essay does not take up Foucault's *The Use of Pleasure* and *The Care of the Self*. Foucault attempts to resolve the genealogical problems I am discussing in this essay with a problematic pastoral move in volumes 2 and 3, where the body of the Greek homosexual comes to stand for an aesthetic unity. My reading of volumes 2 and 3 is influenced by Suzanne Gearhard, "The Taming of Michel Foucault: New Historicism, Psychoanalysis, and the Subversion of Power." *New Literary History* 28 (1997): 457–80.

21. Foucault, *Discipline and Punish*, esp. 13–17.

22. See Michel de Certeau, *The Practice of Everyday Life*, trans. Steven Rendall (Berkeley: University of California Press, 1984), 45–76; Homi K. Bhabha, "'Race,' Time, and the Revision of Modernity," in *The Location of Culture* (New York: Routledge, 1994), 236–56; Eve Kosofsky Sedgwick, *Epistemology of the Closet* (Berkeley: University of California Press, 1990), 45.

23. De Certeau, *Practice*, 64.

24. Bhabha, "'Race,'" 248.

25. I am inspired by Sedgwick's critique of historicism in her *Epistemology*, which she passionately summarizes on pages 46–47. See also Joan Wallach Scott, "After History?" *Common Knowledge* 5 (1996): 8–26; and Graham Hammill, *Sexuality and Form: Caravaggio, Marlowe, and Bacon* (Chicago: University of Chicago Press, 2000).

26. Foucault, *History*, vol. 1, 147.

27. Foucault, *History*, vol. 1, 148; emphasis in original.

28. Ann Laura Stoler, *Race and the Education of Desire: Foucault's History of Sexuality and the Colonial Order of Things* (Durham, N.C.: Duke University Press, 1995).

29. Homi Bhabha, "Of Mimicry and Man: The Ambivalence of Colonial Discourse," in his *Location of Culture*, 86.

30. See my essay that describes how in 1366 the English crown both juridically fabricated the notion of English and Irish blood and then prohibited relations on that basis: "The Cut of Genealogy: Pedagogy in the Blood," *Journal of Medieval and Renaissance Studies*, special issue on "Decolonizing the Middle Ages," 30, 3 (Fall 2000): 449–62; for a discursive reflection on the "purity of blood" laws in Spain see Marc Shell, "From Coexistence to Toleration; or, Marranos (Pigs) in Spain," in his *Children of the Earth: Literature, Politics, and Nationhood* (New York: Oxford University Press, 1993), 224–40. Henry Kamen offers a discussion and bibliographic guide to limpieza de sangre (purity of blood) legislation in Spain in his *The Spanish Inquisition: A Historical Revision* (New Haven, Conn.: Yale University Press, 1997).

31. Michel Foucault, *The Archaeology of Knowledge and the Discourse on Language*, trans. A. M. Sheridan Smith (New York: Harper and Row, 1972), 28.

32. Dominick LaCapra, "Rereading Foucault's 'History of Madness'" in his *History and Reading: Tocqueville, Foucault, French Studies* (Toronto: University of Toronto Press, 2000), 144.

33. Foucault, "Nietzsche, Genealogy, History," 154.

Chapter 4. Lachrymose History, the Typological Imaginary, and the Lacanian Enlightenment

1. Moses Mendelssohn, *Jerusalem and Other Jewish Writings*, trans. Alfred Jospe (New York: Schocken Books, 1969): 74 (epigraph p. 91, emphasis mine). A rich literature on the Haskalah and its aftermath informs this chapter; the following can serve as examples only: Amos Funkenstein, *Perceptions of Jewish History* (Berkeley: University of California Press, 1993); Sander L. Gilman, *Jewish Self-Hatred: Anti-Semitism and the Hidden Language of Jews* (Baltimore: Johns Hopkins University Press, 1986); Jeffrey S. Librett, *The Rhetoric of Cultural Dialogue: Jews and Germans from Moses Mendelssohn to Richard Wagner and Beyond* (Stanford, Calif.: Stanford University Press, 2000); Michael A. Meyer, *The Origins of the Modern Jew: Jewish Identity and European Culture in Germany 1749–1824* (Detroit: Wayne State University Press, 1967); idem, *Response to Modernity: A History of the Reform Movement in Judaism* (New York: Oxford University Press, 1988); idem, ed., *German-Jewish History in Modern Times*, vol. 1, *Tradition and Enlightenment, 1600–1780* (New York: Columbia University Press, 1996); David Sorkin, *The Berlin Haskalah and German Religious Thought: Orphans of Knowledge* (London: Valentine Mitchell, 2000). The volume *German-Jewish History* includes a useful bibliographical essay (393–402).

2. Mendelssohn, *Jerusalem*, 97.

3. "And the characters of the Trauerspiel die, because it is only thus, as corpses, that they can enter the homeland of allegory," Walter Benjamin, *The Origin of German Tragic Drama*, trans. by John Osborne (New York: Verso, 1977), 217.

4. Robert Liberles, *Salo Wittmayer Baron: Architect of Jewish History* (New York: New York University Press, 1995). Baron is noted for his eighteen-volume *A Social and Religious History of the Jews* (New York: Columbia University Press, 1952). See David Nirenberg, *Communities of Violence: Persecution of Minorities in the Middle Ages* (Princeton, N.J.: Princeton University Press, 1996); and, Miri Rubin, *Gentile Tales: The Narrative Assault on Late Medieval Jews* (New Haven, Conn.: Yale University Press, 1999). I should note that in their discussions of lachrymosity Rubin does not cite Baron, nor does Nirenberg. Rubin does cite Nirenberg and lists the work of Gavin Langmuir, *Toward a Definition of Antisemitism* (Berkeley: University of California Press, 1990), as an example of lachrymose history.

5. For a nuanced study of the iteration of the term "state within a state" see Jacob Katz, "A State Within a State: The History of an Anti-Semitic Slogan," in *Zur Assimilation und Emanzipation der Juden* (Darmstadt: Wissenschaftliche Buchgesellschaft, 1982), 124–53.

6. Salo Wittmayer Baron, "Ghetto and Emancipation: Shall We Revise the Traditional View?" *Menorah Journal* 14 (June 1928): 515–26, see 525 for "Dark Ages." Although he warned against nostalgia for the Ghetto, Baron encouraged Jewish cultural renewal and urged "modern" scholars of his generation

to return to Hebrew studies. Such a revival was in self-conscious rejection of "Germanizing" aspects of Wissenschaft des Judentums. His essay is without notes, but presumably he had in mind the work of scholars such as Franz Rosenzweig, who died in the year that Baron was appointed to the chair in Jewish Studies at Columbia University. For exciting new studies of Rosenzweig, see Paul Mendes-Flohr, *German Jews: A Dual Identity* (New Haven, Conn.: Yale University Press, 1999) and Eric L. Santner, *On the Psychotheology of Everyday Life: Reflections on Freud and Rosenzweig* (Chicago: University of Chicago Press, 2001).

7. Baron, "Ghetto and Emancipation," 526.

8. For the inspiration of postcolonial critique, see Daniel Boyarin, "'Épater l'embourgeoisement': Freud, Gender, and the (De)Colonized Psyche," *Diacritics* 24 (1994): 17–41; and Susannah Heschel, *Abraham Geiger and the Jewish Jesus* (Chicago: University of Chicago Press, 1998), 2–3 and passim.

9. Nirenberg, *Communities of Violence*, 4.

10. Miri Rubin discusses the lament on p. 139 of her *Gentile Tales*. Her translation may be found on pp. 196–98.

11. See Jakob J. Petuchowski, *Prayerbook Reform in Europe: The Liturgy of European Liberal and Reform Judaism* (New York: World Union for Progressive Judaism, 1968), 5, for the fate of this liturgical poem.

12. Cited in Petuchowski, *Prayerbook Reform*, 130–43.

13. Petuchowski, *Prayerbook Reform*, 109.

14. See David Philipson, *The Reform Movement in Judaism*, 2nd ed. (New York: Macmillan, 1931); and Myer, *Response to Modernity*.

15. The guiding principles of the Verein der Reformfreunde founded in Frankfurt in 1842 contain such declarations of faith (see Philipson, *Reform Movement*, 118).

16. Leopold Zunz, *Die Gottesdienstlichen Vorträge der Juden* (Berlin: A. Asher, 1832), 401 (Daher blieb die Sprache dieser Dichter meist schwer, dunkel, selbst räthselhaft . . . Inhalt und Künstlichkeit des Baues machen daher dieser Piutim unübersetzbar). For a recent overview of research, see Stefan C. Reif, *Judaism and Hebrew Prayer: New Perspectives on Jewish Liturgical History* (New York: Cambridge University Press, 1993). The appreciation of Spanish liturgical and love poetry over against Ashkenazi poetry is marked in this literature, "Compared with the extraordinary richness and variety of Spanish poetry, that of the other European countries appears narrow and confined"; Salo Wittmayer Baron, *Hebrew Language and Letters*, vol. 7 (New York, Columbia University Press, 1958), 175.

17. This statement of Steinschneider's was reported by Gotthold Weil, "Moritz Steinschneider," *Jüdische Rundschau* 12, 6 (1907): 54 (Wir haben nur noch die Aufgabe, die Überreste des Judentums ehrenvoll zu bestatten').

18. Salo Wittmayer Baron, "Moritz Steinschneider's Contributions to Jewish Historiography," in *History and Jewish Historians* (Philadelphia: Jewish Publication Society, 1964), 451, nn. 449–70 ("traurigen Themas").

19. Mladen Dolar, "'I Shall Be with You on Your Wedding-Night': Lacan and the Uncanny," *October* 58 (1991): 5–23; Joan Copjec, *Read My Desire: Lacan Against the Historicists* (Cambridge, Mass.: MIT Press, 1994); and Slavoj Žižek, *The Ticklish Subject: The Absent Centre of Political Ontology* (New York: Verso, 1999).

20. For a discussion of the kind of work that needs to be done in reading Kant together with Mendelssohn, see Librett, *The Rhetoric of Cultural Dialogue*,

24–35; Sorkin, *The Berlin Haskalah*; Jacques Derrida, "Interpretations at War: Kant, the Jew, the German," *New Literary History* 22 (1991): 39–95. Also Santner's important discussion of Rosenzweig's relation to Wissenschaft des Judentums in his *On the Psychotheology of Everyday Life*.

21. See Sigmund Freud, "Das Unheimliche," in *Gesammelte Werke* [*GW*], vol. 12 (Frankfurt: Fischer, 1947), 229–67; and translated by Joan Riviere, "The Uncanny," *Collected Works of Sigmund Freud*, vol. 4 (London: Hogarth Press, 1956), 368–407. Also see "Der Mann Moses und die Monotheistiche Religion," in *GW*, vol. 16 (Frankfurt: Fischer, 1950), 103–246; in translation in *Moses and Monotheism, Standard Edition of the Collected Works* [*SE*], trans. Katherine Jones (New York: Vintage, 1967). Yosef Hayim Yerushalmi, *Freud's Moses: Judaism Terminable and Interminable* (New Haven, Conn.: Yale University Press, 1991) is also invaluable.

22. Citation (Was unsterblich im Sesang soll leben, muß im Leben untergehen) Freud, *GW*, 16: 208; *Moses*, 130. I am reading Freud with recent suggestive work on Echo, ethics, and iteration. Freud leaves Echo out of his studies of narcissism; see Gayatri Chakravorty Spivak, "Echo," in *The Spivak Reader*, ed. Donna Landry and Gerald MacLean (New York: Routledge, 1996), 175–203; Denise Riley, *The Words of Selves: Identification, Solidarity, Irony* (Stanford, Calif.: Stanford University Press, 2000), 146–84; Joan W. Scott, "Fantasy Echo: History and the Construction of Identity," *Critical Inquiry* 27 (2001), 284–35.

23. Freud, *The Interpretation of Dreams*, trans. Joyce Crick (Oxford: Oxford University Press, 1999), 382.

24. The images of this dream remind us of the terrifying children of the Sandman, a story that Freud might have read as a child and which serves as a core subject of his analysis in his essay on the uncanny: "his children, who sit in a nest and have crooked beaks like owls with which they pick up the eyes of human children who have been naughty." I am using the German text *E. T. A. Hoffmann: der Sandmann*, ed. Ulrich Hohoff (New York: Walter de Gruyter, 1988), "fur seine Kinderchen, die sitzen dort im Nest, und haben krumme Schnäbel, wie die Eulen, damit picken sie der unartigen Menschenkindlein Augen auf," 7. For the English text see E. T. A. Hoffmann, *Selected Writings of E.T.A. Hoffmann*, ed. and trans. Leonard J. Kent and Elizabeth C. Knight (Chicago: University of Chicago Press, 1969).

25. Freud, *SE*, 4: 277–78. Freud does not mention "silent pictures" in his work on dreams but he certainly would have known of this technology as he wrote this book. Freud encountered serial photography during his trip to Paris in 1885–86. At Salpêtrière Albert Londe used serial cameras to anatomize the hysterical arc of Charcot's subjects. By 1909, such serial photographs could be projected as films. See Friedrich A. Kittler, *Discourse Networks 1800/1900*, trans. Michael Metteer (Palo Alto: Stanford University Press, 1990). The Brothers Skladanowsky were already showing their "lebenden Photographien" (15 minute long silent features) in Berlin by 1895, see Ludwig Greve, Margot Pehle, and Heidi Westhoff, eds., *Hätte ich das Kino! Die Schriftsteller und der Stummfilm* (Marbach: Schiller-Nationalmuseum, 1976), 14.

26. Mladen Dolar, " The Object Voice," in *Gaze and Voice as Love Objects*, ed. Renata Salecl and Slavoj Žižek (Durham, N.C.: Duke University Press, 1996), 15. Dolar imagines a kind of acoustical echo within the very voicing of narcissistic satisfaction: "that at the very core of narcissism there lies an alien kernel that the narcissistic satisfaction may well attempt to disguise, but which continually threatens to undermine it from the inside."

27. Peter Gay, *Freud: A Life for Our Time* (New York: W.W. Norton, 1988) provides biographical details on Freud's mother, Amalia Nathansohn Freud (504), on Jakob Freud's speaking Hebrew "as well as German or better" (6), and on his nurse (7). On Freud and Yiddish see Christopher Hutton, "Freud and the Family Drama of Yiddish," in *Studies in Yiddish Linguistics*, ed. Paul Wexler (Tübingen: Max Niemeyer Verlag, 1990), 8–22. Freud's anxiety about languages heard in the nursery also affected his analysis of the Wolf Man. He missed the dream cryptonomy of this analysand by not realizing that English (and not German) was the language of his nursery.The importance of nursery languages in dream cryptonomy has been brilliantly analyzed by Nicolas Abraham and Maria Torok, *The Wolf Man's Magic Word: A Cryptonomy*, trans. Nicholas Rand (Minneapolis: University of Minnesota Press, 1986).

28. "We shall venture, therefore, to refer the uncanny effect of the Sand-Man to the child's dread in relation to its castration-complex," *SE*, 385. ("Wir würden es also wagen, das Unheimliche des Sandmannes auf die Angst des kindlichen Kastrationskomplexes zuruckführen" [*GW* 245]).

29. Freud, "Uncanny," 399.

30. Citations from *E. T. A. Hoffmann: der Sandmann*, ed. Hohoff.

31. Hoffman, *Selected Writings*, 105. "Was See-was Spiegel! Können wir denn das Mädchen anschauen, ohne daß uns aus ihrem Blick wunderbare himmische Gesänge und Klänge entgegenstrahlen, die in unser Innerstes dringen, daß da alles wach und rege wird? Singen wir selbst dann nichts wahrhaft gescheutes, so is überhaupt nicht viel an uns, und das lesen wir denn auch deutlich in dem um Claras Lippen schwebenden feinen Lächeln, wenn wir uns unterfangen, ihr etwas vorzuquinkeliren, das so tun will als sei es Gesang, unerachtet nur einzelne Töne verworren durch einander springen" (Hoffman, *E. T. A. Hoffmann: der Sandmann*, 64–65).

32. Friedrich A. Kittler, *Discourse Networks 1800/1900*, trans. Michael Metteer (Stanford, Calif.: Stanford University Press, 1990). I think that Hoffmann's story performs the gap in this network, whence its uncanniness. See Kittler, *Discourse Networks*.

33. Kittler, *Discourse Networks*, 33.

34. Kittler, *Discourse Networks* 35.

35. Spivak's essay, "Echo," is helpful in analyzing the significance of this new pedagogy around 1800.

36. Gay, *Freud: A Life for Our Time* provides background on Freud's childhood education. Also his sister recalled that "normally children in old Austria attended a primary or public school for four years, beginning at the age of six, before entering high school. But Sigmund never went to such a school. My father taught him privately until he entered high school, where he headed his class through all the eight years' course." Anna Freud Bernays, "My Brother Sigmund Freud," in *Freud as We Knew Him*, ed. Hendrik M. Ruitenbeck (Detroit: Wayne State University Press, 1973), 141.

37. Sorkin, *The Berlin Haskalah* describes how Mendelssohn made the Hebrew accents the chief guide to literary meaning (97). I am trying to find out more about the specific kind of spelling and/or syllabic pedagogy that Jakob Freud would have encountered as he learned Hebrew and as he attempted to teach it.

38. Friedrich Kittler, *Gramophone, Film, Typewriter,* trans. Geoffrey Winthrop-Young and Michael Wutz (Stanford, Calif.: Stanford University Press, 1999), 55–69, traces the relations of the phonetic system of reading to the sacred

duty of the state. Steven Beller, *Vienna and the Jews, 1867–1938: A Cultural History* (New York: Cambridge University Press, 1989), 88–105, describes the kind of hybrid education that a child like Freud would have had in Vienna. My study is intended to join and amplify Sander L. Gilman's crucial study of language in *Jewish Self-Hatred: Anti-Semitism and the Hidden Language of the Jews* (Baltimore: Johns Hopkins University Press, 1986). Please note that I am not implying some gendered story of Yiddish as a feminine language. I am only arguing for a gender reversal and its implications in the teaching of the "national" language (German) to Freud in his childhood.

39. Consider in contrast Walt Whitman's rhapsody for the throat—"Oh throat! Oh trembling throat!" Here it is useful to crisscross Freud's use of Goethe as a ventriloquist in the study by Sabine Prokhoris, *The Witch's Kitchen: Freud, Faust, and the Transference*, trans. G. M. Goshgarian (Ithaca, N.Y.: Cornell University Press, 1995) with suggestive thoughts about voice and throat to be found in Wayne Koestenbaum, *The Queen's Throat: Opera, Homosexuality, and the Mystery of Desire* (New York: Poseidon, 1993). Koestenbaum draws attention to Walt Whitman's poetry (14).

40. Freud, "Uncanny," 385.

41. Yerushalmi translates this Hebrew inscription in his *Freud's Moses*, 105. An inspiring reading of *Moses and Monotheism* can be found in Santner, *Psychotheology*. Also see Daniel Boyarin, "'An Imaginary and Desirable Converse': *Moses and Monotheism* as Family Romance," in *Reading Bibles, Writing Bodies*, Identity and the Book, ed. Timothy K. Beal and David M. Gunn (New York: Routledge, 1997), 184–207; Jay Geller, "A Paleontological View of Freud's Study of Religion: Unearthing the *Leitfossil* of Circumcision," *Modern Judaism* 13 (1993): 49–70; Julia Reinhard Lupton, "*Ethnos* and Circumcision in the Pauline Tradition: A Psychoanalytic Exegesis," in *The Psychoanalysis of Race*, ed. Christopher Lane (New York: Columbia University Press, 1998), 193–210.

42. Freud, *SE*, 116; *GW*, 198.

43. Freud, *SE*, 156. "Die Beschneidung ist der symbolische Ersatz der Kastration, die der Urvater einst aus der Fülle seiner Machtvollkommenheit über die Söhne verhängt hatte, und wer dies Symbol annahm, zeigte damit, daß er bereit war, sich dem Willlen des Vaters zu unterwefen, auch wenn er ihm das schmerzlichste Opfer auferlegte"; *GW*, 230.

44. Discussion of circumcision occurs as follows (first page number refers to *SE*, second page number refers to *GW*): 29, 125; 33, 128; 35, 129; 40, 134; 46, 139; 47, 139; 47, 140; 53, 144; 54, 145; 74, 163; 76, 165; 112, 194; 116, 198; 156, 230.

45. Freud, *SE*, 63; *GW*, 153. See *Moses* and *GW* for similar citations: 80, 167; 85, 172; 86, 173.

46. Freud, *SE*, 80; *GW*, 167. *SE*, 85. "Was in der Niederschrifft ausgellasen oder abgeändert worden war, konnte sehr wohl in der Tradition unversehrt erhalten geblieben sein."

47. "Eindrücke aus der Zeit der beginnenden Sprachfähigkeit heben sic als besonders interessant hervor"; Freud, *SE*, 93; *GW* 179.

48. Freud, *SE*, 93; *GW*, 179.

49. Freud, *SE*, 12. "Hier scheint also ein gesicherter Fall von archaischer Erbschaft aus der Zeit der Sprachentwicklung"; *GW*, 206.

50. Freud, *SE*, 46; *GW*, 139.

51. Julia Reinhard Lupton, *Afterlives of the Saints: Hagiography, Typology, and Renaissance Literature* (Stanford, Calif.: Stanford University Press, 1996), xxi.

Chapter 5. Translating the Foreskin

An earlier version of this essay appeared in *Queering the Middle Ages*, ed. Glenn Burger and Steven F. Kruger (Minneapolis: University of Minnesota Press, 2001). Glenn Burger and Steven Kruger served as editors for this essay in the most generous and capacious sense of that term.

1. Since John Boswell, *The Kindness of Strangers* (New York: Pantheon, 1991), 113, n. 76, noted this lacuna, some thought-provoking new work has appeared: see Shaun F. Tougher, "Byzantine Eunuchs: An Overview, with Special Reference to Their Creation and Origin," in *Women, Men, and Eunuchs: Gender in Byzantium*, ed. Liz James (New York: Routledge, 1998), 168–84. Shaun Marmon discusses medieval eunuchs in Islamic society in *Eunuchs and Sacred Boundaries in Islamic Society* (New York: Oxford University Press, 1995). See also Carolyn Dinshaw, "Eunuch Hermeneutics," in her *Chaucer's Sexual Poetics* (Madison: University of Wisconsin Press, 1989), 156–86.

2. Histories of sexuality, in spite of a seemingly growing impulse to categorize, have mostly avoided a consideration of eunuchs. Foucault's (through Nietzsche) rhetorical disdain of the eunuch has certainly helped to place eunuchs under the sign of abjection. Eve Kosofsky Sedgwick has written eloquently about the impulse to categorize as a guarantee of the epistemology of the closet, *Epistemology of the Closet* (Berkeley: University of California Press, 1990). A worrying tendency to categorize comes into view in the important review essay by David M. Halperin, "Forgetting Foucault: Acts, Identities, and the History of Sexuality," *Representations* 63 (1998): 93–120.

3. I discuss Foucault and eunuchs more fully in Chapter 3 (see note 20 for full references). Foucault cites Nietzsche in his discussion of genealogical history: "I can't stand these lustful eunuchs of history, all the seductions of the ascetic ideal; I can't stand these whited sepulchres producing life or those tired and indifferent beings who dress up in the part of wisdom and adopt an objective point of view"; "Nietzsche, Genealogy, History," in *Language, Counter-Memory, Practice*, trans. Donald Bouchard (Ithaca, N.Y.: Cornell University Press, 1977), 138–64.

4. Amitav Ghosh, *In an Antique Land* (New York: Knopf, 1993). James Clifford opens his recent book, *Routes*, with a discussion of Ghosh's ethnography as the exemplification of the transcultural predicaments of the late twentieth century, in particular, as they bear on the struggles and arts of cultural encounter. Relevant to Ghosh's study is the memoir of a Jewish childhood and family history told by André Aciman, *Out of Egypt: A Memoir* (New York: Farrar, Straus, Giroux, 1994).

5. Sigmund Freud, "Fetishism," in *Collected Papers*, ed. James Strachey, vol. 5 (New York: Basic Books, 1959), 198–204; the citation is on 198.

6. Freud, "Fetishism," 198.

7. Freud, "Fetishism," 201.

8. My reading of Freud's essay relies on the following: Daniel Boyarin, "'Épater l'embourgeoisement': Freud, Gender, and the (De)Colonized Psyche," *Diacritics* 24 (1994): 17–41; Jay Geller, "'A Glance at the Nose': Freud's Inscription of Jewish Difference," *American Imago* 49 (1992): 445–66; and Sander Gilman, *Freud, Race, and Gender* (Princeton, N.J.: Princeton University Press, 1993).

9. Gilman, *Freud, Race, and Gender*, 39.

10. Boyarin, "'Épater l'embourgeoisement,'" 38.

11. See Geller, "'A Glance at the Nose.'"

12. William Pietz, "The Problem of the Fetish," *Res: A Journal of Aesthetics and Anthropology* 9 (1985): 5–17; 13 (1987): 23–45; 16 (1988): 105–23.

13. Pietz, "The Problem of the Fetish," 35.

14. Anne McClintock, *Imperial Leather: Race, Gender, and Sexuality in Colonial Contest* (New York: Routledge, 1995), 184.

15. McClintock, *Imperial Leather*, 21.

16. Ghosh, *In an Antique Land*, 33. Ghosh bases his study partly on what is called the Cairo Geniza archive. The Hebrew word *geniza* meaning storage, hiding, or burial place has become familiar to medievalists as the name given to the cache of several thousand documents, mostly composed in medieval Arabic and written in the Hebrew alphabet, which accumulated for centuries in a silo-like room, called the *geniza*, in the important synagogue located in Fustat, Cairo.

17. Ghosh, *In an Antique Land*, 60.

18. Ghosh, *In an Antique Land*, 61.

19. Ghosh, *In an Antique Land*, 62. Ghosh's failure to recognize the word for sex and his impurity reduce him to the one "who does not know" in the eyes of the young male villagers. In another bout of teasing, the village boys say: "Shouldn't we tell him? . . . How's he going to grow up if he doesn't 'beat the ten'?" A village boy responds: "It's no use. He won't understand—he doesn't know a thing. Look I'll show you" (64). The village boys then go on to test Ghosh's very command of the visible world by asking him to identify the source of a reflection on a field-canal. I am grateful to my colleague Patrick Gaffney for help in going over the words *darab* (to strike, to beat) and *assar* (to copulate). Also, see Socrates Spiro, *Arabic-English Dictionary of the Colloquial Arabic of Egypt* (London: B. Quaritch, 1895).

20. Ghosh, *In an Antique Land*, 203.

21. The slippage of circumcision and clitoridectomy, which is implicit in Ghosh, recalls the arguments made by Gilman, *Freud, Race, and Gender*. See also Kaja Silverman, "Historical Trauma and Male Subjectivity," in her *Male Subjectivity at the Margins* (New York: Routledge, 1992), 52–121. Her study provides an argument thinking about clitoridectomy as an embodied form of traumatic memory doing the work of binding for the phallic fiction: "The verb 'to bind' has a very specific sense in Freud's writings. It refers not only to the circumscription of a homeostatic body of energy within the limits of the ego, but the processes whereby memories characterized by a high degree of affective and sensory intensity are brought within linguistic control—the process whereby they are anchored to signifiers, and consequently to meaning. The memories in question are totally transformed by this binding operation; indeed, it might be more accurate to say that something else is put in the place of the original, hallucinatory mnemic traces" (65).

22. Ghosh, *In an Antique Land*, 246.

23. Ghosh, *In an Antique Land*, 254.

24. Ghosh, *In an Antique Land*, 261.

25. Ghosh, *In an Antique Land*, 263.

26. S. D. Goitein's work on the Cairo Geniza archive, as Ghosh suggests, deeply inspired him (Ghosh just missed meeting Goitein before the latter's death in 1985). Goitein is the editor of the five-volume study based on documents from the Cairo Geniza, *A Mediterranean Society: The Jewish Communities of the Arab World* (Berkeley: University of California Press, 1967–88).

I will concentrate here primarily on his earlier work, *Jews and Arabs: Their Contacts Through the Middle Ages* (New York: Schocken Books, 1955). More recently the study by Elinoar Bareket has appeared: *The Jewish Elite in Medieval Egypt* (Leiden: Brill, 1999). For an enabling reading of the complexities of Goitein's Zionism, see Ammiel Alcalay, *After Jews and Arabs: Remaking Levantine Culture* (Minneapolis: University of Minnesota Press, 1993); and, more broadly, the essays in the following collection: Benjamin Hary, John L. Hayes, and Fred Astren, eds., *Judaism and Islam: Boundaries, Communication, and Interaction, Essays in Honor of William M. Brinner* (New York: Brill, 2000).

27. Goitein, *Jews and Arabs*, 27.

28. Goitein, *Jews and Arabs*, 27.

29. Goitein, *Jews and Arabs*, 28.

30. Goitein, *Jews and Arabs*, 104.

31. The question of slavery in the medieval world has too often been approached from the perspective of Marc Bloch: how did the slavery of the antique world come to an end? See his *Slavery and Serfdom in the Middle Ages: Selected Essays*, trans. William R. Beer (Berkeley: University of California Press, 1975). Such an agenda has ignored the evidence of slavery's centrality in the production of the so-called "bourgeois revolution" described by Goitein in his *Jews and Arabs* (100). For the reticence of medieval studies in dealing with medieval slavery, see the essays in Allen J. Frantzen and Douglas Moffat, ed., *The Work of Work: Servitude, Slavery and Labor in Medieval England* (Glasgow: Cruithne Press, 1994). See also Ruth Mazo Karras, *Slavery and Society in Medieval Scandinavia* (New Haven, Conn.: Yale University Press, 1988), who questions the so-called "break" between medieval slavery and Enlightenment systems of slavery. The fact that, in the abiding shadow of Pirenne and his thesis delineated in *Mohammed and Charlemagne*, trans. Bernard Miall (New York: Barnes and Noble, 1958), Europe and Islam are discussed as separate entities in economic histories enables the resistance to dealing with large-scale slave exchanges in the world economy of the ninth through the twelfth centuries. For exciting work that is reopening the question of medieval slavery in fresh new ways, see Benjamin Braude, "The Sons of Noah and the Construction of Ethnic and Geographical Identities in the Medieval and Early Modern Periods," *William and Mary Quarterly* 54 (1997): 103–43; Susan Mosher Stuard, "Ancillary Evidence for the Decline of Medieval Slavery," *Past and Present* 149 (1995): 3–28; and Olivia Remie Constable, "Muslim Spain and Mediterranean Slavery: The Medieval Slave Trade as an Aspect of Muslim-Christian Relations," in *Christendom and Its Discontents: Exclusion, Persecution, and Rebellion, 1000–1500*, ed. Scott Waugh (Cambridge: Cambridge University Press, 1995), 264–84.

32. Philip Curtin, *Cross-Cultural Trade in World History* (Baltimore: Johns Hopkins University Press, 1984), 107.

33. Richard Hodges and David Whitehouse, *Mohammed, Charlemagne, and the Origins of Europe* (Ithaca, N.Y.: Cornell University Press, 1983). For the scale of exchange, see especially the sections on Baghdad, Samarra, and the major Indian Ocean sites of Siraf, Kilwa, and Zanzibar that flourished during this period (123–57). The traditional argument that medieval slavery was on a "different scale" from the early modern is in need of careful reevaluation.

34. Maurice Lombard, *The Golden Age of Islam*, trans. Joan Spencer (New York: Elsevier, 1975), 195.

35. For the etymology of this word in Arabic and European sources where

it appears as a borrowed word by the thirteenth century, see Charles Ver-linden, "L'Origine de sclavus-esclave," *Bulletin du Cange* 17 (1943): 7–128; also his "Encore sur les origines de sclavus-esclave," *L'Esclavage dans l'Europe médiévale*, vol. 2 (Ghent: Rijksuniversiteit te Gent, 1977), 999–1010; David Ayalon, "On the Eunuchs of Islam," *Jerusalem Studies in Arabic and Islam* 1 (1979): 67–124; Henry Kahane and Renee Kahane, "Notes on the Linguistic History of Sclavus," *Studi in Onore di Ettore Lo Gatto e Giovanni Mauer,* Collan di Richerche slavistiche (Florence: Sansoni, 1962), 345–60; and Daniel Pipes, *Slave Soldiers and Islam: The Genesis of a Military System* (New Haven, Conn.: Yale University Press, 1981), 99.

36. Ghosh, *In an Antique Land*, 262.

37. Pipes, *Slave Soldiers and Islam*, 99.

38. Goitein, *Jews and Arabs*, 15.

39. Goitein, *Jews and Arabs*, 15.

40. Marmon, *Eunuchs*, 63.

41. See Hortense J. Spillers, "Mama's Baby, Papa's Maybe: An American Grammar Book," *Diacritics* 17 (1987): 65–81.

42. The Golden Age constructed by Goitein and Ghosh might even be thought of as an orientalism in reverse: see Sadiq Jalal al-'Azm, "Orientalism and Orientalism in Reverse," in *Forbidden Agendas: Intolerance and Defiance in the Middle East*, ed. John Rothschild (London: Al Saqui Books, 1984), 349–75.

43. Partha Chatterjee, *The Nation and Its Fragments: Colonial and Postcolonial Histories* (Princeton, N.J.: Princeton University Press, 1993), 102.

44. Chatterjee, *The Nation and Its Fragments*, 110.

45. Chatterjee, *The Nation and Its Fragments*, 110.

46. Teresa de Lauretis, *The Practices of Love: Lesbian Sexuality and Perverse Desire* (Bloomington: Indiana University Press, 1994), 231.

47. De Lauretis, *The Practices of Love*, 231.

Index

Page numbers in italics indicate illustrations.

Acknowledgments

Hospitality, academic and domestic, has attended the unfolding of this project. In 1998–99, Keith Baker, Director of the Stanford Humanities Center, and Susan Dunn, Associate Director, provided me with a vibrant academic home during my fellowship year. I am grateful to them, to the excellent staff of the Humanities Center, and to its residents that year, both faculty and graduate students, for helping me to shape this book. Likewise, the associate deans of the Institute for Scholarship in the Liberal Arts at the University of Notre Dame, Julia Douthwaite, and her successor, Cindy Bergeman, have always encouraged me to seek and find. They have generously defrayed the publication of figures and the compilation of the index for this book. The librarians in the Medieval Institute of the University of Notre Dame, especially Marina Smyth and Linda Major, and the manager of Interlibrary Loan, Linda Gregory, patiently and unflaggingly assisted me. I am likewise grateful to the staff of the Rare Books Collections at the New York Public Library and at the British Library for access to their materials. Renee Hall, librarian of the Media Lab Europe (Dublin), assisted me with procuring materials for final revisions during my visit there at Fulbright Fellow. Her graceful fielding of my requests (amidst those from electrical engineers and multi-media artists) reminds me of the capacious resilience of the library as an institution.

My interlocutors at Notre Dame, Doris Bergen, Mary Rose D'Angelo, Jill Godmilow, and Graham Hammill, never let me stop too soon. Other colleagues beyond Notre Dame have always welcomed discussion and at one time or another have offered me their invaluable editorial comments. Thanks to Judith Bennett, Glenn Burger, Michael Camille (dear colleague, now sadly deceased), Sealy Gilles, Michal Kobialka, Steven Kruger, Lisa Rofel, Helen Solterer, Sylvia Tomasch, and Kerry Walk. I also wish to thank my undergraduate students at Notre Dame for their exuberant willingness to explore themes of this book in their studies with me.

Generous domestic hospitality eased the work of this book. I have dedicated it to my partner and engaged interlocutor, Bob Franklin, who did not live to see its completion. As I continued my research after his death, other hearths welcomed me. In particular, Peter Bury and his daughters, Francesca and Eleanor, opened their house to me during my research in London. They never cease to surprise me with their capaciousness. I owe special thanks, too, to my personal friends who know what hospitality without calculation means: C.C. Bethe, Dicky and Georgey Daskais, Mary Gordon, Sean Keilen and Marty Rojas, Esther and Alan Sax, Naomi Stern and Jack Jaffe.

How fortunate I am that this manuscript came to the door of the University of Pennsylvania Press. My editors, Jerome Singerman and Rebecca Rich, embrace hospitality toward their authors. I am indebted to their editorial concerns that this book be hospitable to its readers. Where my book fails in this, it is not due to their want of generosity and patience.

The following presses have permitted me to reprint revised forms of earlier essays. Chapter 1 appeared in an early version as "The ABC of Ptolemy: Mapping the World with the Alphabet," in *Text and Territory: Geographical Imagination in the European Middle Ages*, ed. Sealy Gilles and Sylvia Tomasch (Philadelphia: University of Pennsylvania Press, 1998), 223–41. Chapter 2 is a revision of "Becoming Collection: The Spatial Afterlife of Universal Histories, " in *Medieval Spatial Practices*, ed. Barbara A. Hanawalt and Michal Kobialka (Minneapolis: University of Minnesota Press, 2000), 223–41; an essay from *Art Bulletin*, "Paper Jews: Inscription/Ethnicity/Ethnography," 78 (1996): 594–99 is revised to form part of Chapter 3. Chapter 5 is a revised version of "Translating the Foreskin," in *Queering the Middle Ages/Historicizing Postmodernity*, ed. Glenn Burger and Steven F. Kruger (Minneapolis: University of Minnesota Press, 2001), 193–212.